The Rainbow Beneath My Feet

The Rainbow Beneath My Feet

A Mushroom Dyer's Field Guide

Arleen Rainis Bessette & Alan E. Bessette

SYRACUSE UNIVERSITY PRESS

First Edition 2001
22 23 24 25 26 9 8 7 6 5

∞ The paper used in this publication meets the minimum requirements of the American National Standard for Information Sciences—Permanence of Paper for Printed Library Materials, ANSI Z39.48-1992.

For a listing of books published and distributed by Syracuse University Press, visit https://press.syr.edu.

ISBN: 978-0-8156-0680-2

LIBRARY OF CONGRESS CATALOGING-IN-PUBLICATION DATA
Bessette, Arleen Rainis, 1951–
The rainbow beneath my feet : a mushroom dyer's field guide / Arleen Rainis Bessette and Alan E. Bessette. — 1st ed.
p. cm.
Includes bibliographical references (p.).
ISBN: 0-8156-0680-x (pbk. : alk. paper)
I. Dyes and dyeing, Domestic. 2. Mushrooms. I. Bessette, Alan. II. Title

TT854.3 B47 2001
667'.26 — dc21 00–061224

Title page illustration: *Corinarius semisanguineus* with dyed tester strips

Book design by Christopher Kuntze
Manufactured in the United States of America

To MIRIAM C. RICE

For her pioneering work in using mushrooms for color.
Mushroom dyers everywhere will always remain in her debt.

To SUSAN HOPKINS

Friend, mycologist, and dyer extraordinaire.
You opened our eyes to a mycological dimension previously unknown to us.

Susan Hopkins' mushroom-dyed gnomes

Contents

Illustrations ix

Preface xi

Acknowledgements xiii

Mushroom Dyeing: An Introduction 3

General Mushroom Information 5
- Parts of a Mushroom 5
- How to Make a Spore Print 7

Collecting and Preserving Dye Mushrooms 7
- Collecting Clothing and Equipment 9
- When to Collect Mushrooms 9
- Where to Collect Mushrooms 9
- Preserving Dye Mushrooms 11

Dyeing Equipment 11

Preparing the Wool 13

Mordanting 15

Preparing the Dyebath 18

Dyeing the Wool 20

Explanation of the Descriptions of Illustrated Species 23

How to Use the Identification Keys 24

Color Key to the Major Groups of Dye Mushrooms 26

Dye Mushroom Species: Descriptions and Illustrations
- Boletes 35
- Carbon and Cushion Fungi 54
- Chanterelles and Allies 55
- Club Fungi 57
- Coral Fungi 59
- Crust Fungi 59
- Earthstars 61

False Morels 61
Fiber Fans and Vases 63
Gilled Mushrooms 65
Hypomyces 96
Polypores 97
Puffballs and Allies 114
Tooth Fungi 115

Appendixes
A. A Note on Color 157
B. Mushroom Species Dye Color List 159
C. Dye Duds 164

Glossary 165

Bibliography 171

Index 173

Illustrations

Cortinarius semisanguineus with dyed tester strips iii
Susan Hopkins' mushroom-dyed gnomes vi
Arleen Rainis Bessette x
Mushroom dye color ring xii
Crocheted hat made from mushroom-dyed yarn 2
Young stages of *Hydnellum pineticola* 4
Parts of mushrooms 6
Basket of mushrooms 7
Three stages of *Pholiota malicola* and dye test results 8
Hoh Rain Forest 10
Tending the dye pot 12
Close-up of a sheep's face 13
Mushroom-dyed silk scarf 14
Skeins of unmordanted and mordanted yarn 15
Color variation with neutral vs. alkaline dye baths 16
Washing the dyed yarn 17
Preparing the dye bath 18
Dye results from successive afterbaths 19
Checking for color 20
Swinging the skeins 21
Skeins of yarn drying on rack 22
Gymnopilus luteofolius 32
Sarcoscypha austriaca 34
Examples of mushroom-dyed silk 154
Example of varietal variation dye results 157
Vest knitted with mushroom dyed yarn 158
Display at the 8th International Fungi & Fibre Symposium 172

Arleen Rainis Bessette

Preface

THERE HAS BEEN an increased awareness of mushrooms over the past decade, along with a parallel growing interest in "getting back to basics." Recycling, home gardening, wild food gathering, wine and beer making, medicinal uses of plants, and the use of natural fibers for clothing and decoration are but a few areas indicative of this trend. Environmental concerns and a heightened sense of appreciation for the beauty and fragility of this planet with which we coexist may account, in part, for this focus.

My own memory of first collecting mushrooms goes back more than forty years. My grandparents and I collected edible species for the table, although my memory is not of the taste of dishes prepared from the finds of those forays. Rather, my memory is of holding up the brilliant red-capped russulas and the golden and brown-toned boletes for my grandmother's approval. The color and feel of the mushrooms is what remained mind-fast, as memory. Some years later I learned to knit, and discovered the same love of color and texture handling wool that I experienced while collecting mushrooms. This hand-hunger, this need to know the world by touch and feel while simultaneously being transported by the flash and spark of color and form, has been a part of me ever since.

With a background in both science and psychology, I have been fortunate in being able to pursue careers that include mycology and photography in addition to my study of the human psyche. I remain entranced by those elements of the world that engage, delight, and surprise. When a friend introduced me to the concept of dyeing wool with mushrooms, my boundaries of personal history collided and merged with my present-day near obsession with collecting, photographing, writing about, and eating mushrooms. Initially a generational link due to their food value, mushrooms have now gained a unique status as environmentally safe producers of colorfast dyes. Every color is obtainable, from shades of brown and gold to bright reds, oranges, blues, and purples. The process is magical, alchemical, sometimes startling. Imagine the surprise when a nondescript, little brown mushroom transforms a skein of yarn into all the shades of a summer sunset!

Now as I walk through the forests and step deeply into the velvet-cushion mosses, I see so much more than photographic opportunities or tasty dishes waiting to be savored. I gaze down upon the splendor of color and form, awestruck, grateful, mesmerized by the rainbow beneath my feet.

Arleen Rainis Bessette

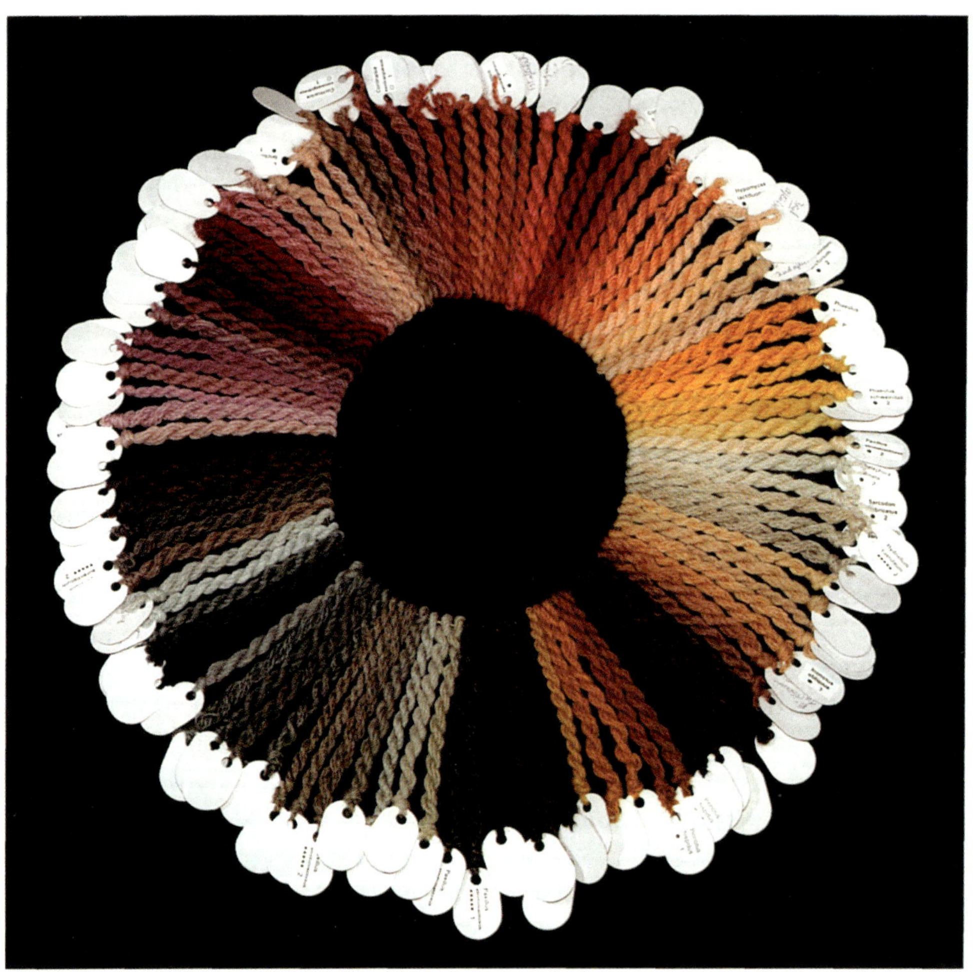

Color ring showing some of the colors obtained dyeing with mushrooms

Acknowledgments

It is with considerable pleasure that we acknowledge the following individuals who have helped us in various ways with this work. For sharing technical data, mycological notes, and preserved specimens, and for assisting in the identification of species, we are grateful to Joseph Ammirati, Tim Baroni, Ernst Both, Phyllis Cole, Dail Dunaway, Ray Fatto, the late Greg Ferguson, Robert Gilbertson, Susan Hopkins, Don Johnston, Steve Trudell, and Nathan Wilson. Valuable collections of fresh mushrooms that we studied and photographed were also contributed by Billie and Ernst Both, Dail Dunaway, the late Greg Ferguson, Jessica and David Harris, Susan Hopkins, Donna Mitchell, Cindy and Peter Molesky, Bill Roody, Nathan Wilson, and Lee Yamada. We appreciate the kindness and hospitality of Lisa Bauer, Billie and Ernst Both, Margaret and Philip Carpenter, Dail and Tina Dunaway, Karen Fogler, Susan Hopkins, and Anna Moore who invited us into their homes and shared their favorite collecting sites with us.

For their photographic and artistic contributions, which greatly enhanced the beauty and utility of this book, we are indebted to Catherine Ardrey, Dail Dunaway, Kenneth M. Evenson, Kenneth J. Harrison, Emily Johnson, Andrew Methven, Orson K. Miller, Jr., Sam Norris, Bill Roody, Walt Sturgeon, Walt Sundberg, and Steve Trudell.

We thank Mattias Andersson, Myra Beebee, Patricia Brannen, Jean Mounter, Samantha Noti, Patricia Olson, Trine Parmer, and Margaret Trussell for graciously allowing photographs of themselves to be included in this work.

We offer heartfelt thanks and appreciation to Susan Hopkins for generously sharing the results of her dyeing experiments, the valuable knowledge she gained from her travels both nationally and internationally, the many hours discussing chemistry and dyeing techniques, and most importantly for first introducing us to the concept of using mushrooms for dyeing.

We thank Bill Roody who read the manuscript and made valuable suggestions for improving the book. We are especially grateful to Dr. Robert Mandel and his staff at Syracuse University Press who made the publication of this book possible.

The Rainbow Beneath My Feet

Crocheted hat: yarn-dyed with *Trametes versicolor*, *Cortinarius semisanguineus*, and *Hapalopilus nidulans*

Mushroom Dyeing: An Introduction

In the early 1970s, Miriam C. Rice first experimented with mushrooms as a possible dye source. Her continued testing, and positive results, were first published in 1974 in her work, *Let's Try Mushrooms for Color.* In 1980, she published her second, more comprehensive work, *Mushrooms For Color.* Since then, interest in using fungi as colorfast and reliable dye sources has grown to an international level, as evidenced by the 1997 8th International Fungi & Fibre Symposium held in Paul Smiths, New York.

Our primary objective in writing this book is to provide a comprehensive reference and field guide to some of the more common and best color-producing dye mushrooms of North America. Our goal is to complement and expand upon Rice's pioneering work by providing color illustrations, detailed species descriptions emphasizing macroscopic features, a balanced representation of eastern and western species, as well as a number of new dye mushrooms not featured in her book.

We have not created new common names for species, believing that scientific nomenclature will be of use to a wider, international audience. We have based each species description on the original published description and have cited the authors accordingly.

Although information on dyeing is provided, this is not intended to be an instructional book on the intricacies of that process. For more complete information on dyeing, we refer the reader to the bibliography. We do hope to provide the reader with enough information and inspiration to begin experimenting with a sound beginner's base.

Young stages of *Hydnellum pineticola*

General Mushroom Information

MUSHROOMS are neither plants nor animals. They belong to their own kingdom, the Kingdom Fungi. Fungi lack chlorophyll and cannot produce food for themselves. They obtain nutrients through a process of external digestion and absorption. Some, as decomposers, extract what they need from dead and decaying materials and are called **saprobes.** Those which attack living plants, animals or other fungi are called **parasites.** The third group exists in a mutually beneficial relationship with living trees or other plants. This relationship is called a **mycorrhizal relationship,** one in which both partners obtain what they need, in part, from the other. Learning which food source, or **substrate,** a particular kind of mushroom requires greatly improves the likelihood of successfully finding it.

Every mushroom that has ever been published has a scientific name, and no two species of mushrooms have the same name. Scientific names always have two parts. The first part is the genus, the first letter of which is always capitalized. The second part is the species name, with all letters in lower case. Due to disagreement among taxonomists, there are discrepancies as to some mushrooms' correct scientific names. Therefore, more than one scientific name may be assigned to a single mushroom.

Parts of a Mushroom

When you are first starting out as a mushroom collector, it is a wise practice to become acquainted with mushroom anatomy since it differs from that of other organisms and may be unfamiliar to you. Refer to the accompanying illustration as you read about the basic macroscopic features described.

The mushroom is a fruiting body that arises from the larger fungal organism which is typically underground or within decaying wood. Imagine a vast underground network of fine filaments that are interconnected and interwoven. When conditions are correct (temperature, moisture, nutrients, pH, daylight length) this living mat, called the **mycelium,** produces an above-ground fruiting body called a mushroom. Mushrooms have seed-like microscopic reproductive structures known as **spores.**

A mushroom begins as an immature form called a **button.** Depending on the species, the button may initially be entirely surrounded by a membranous structure known as the **universal veil.** As the mushroom expands it stretches and tears the universal veil, often leaving remnants on the cap. These remnants are referred to as

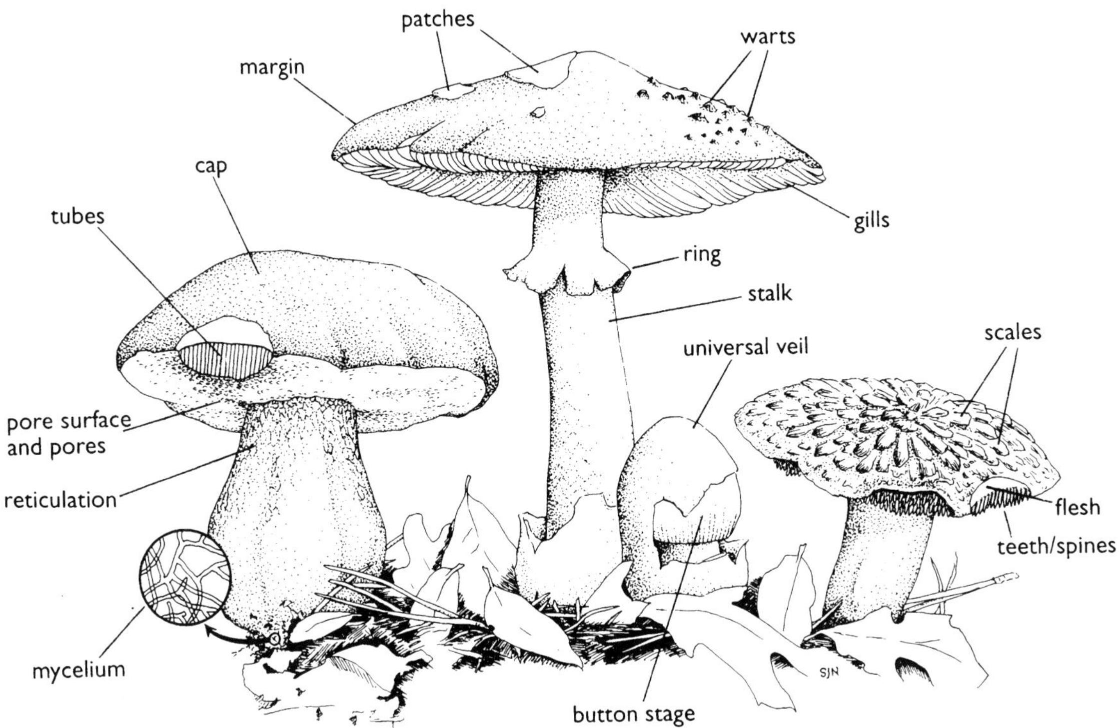

PARTS OF A MUSHROOM

patches or **warts.** There may be a cup-like remnant of the universal veil called a **volva** around the base of the mushroom stalk. Most mushrooms lack a universal veil and therefore have neither patches/warts nor a volva.

Some mature mushrooms have a **cap** and a **stalk.** The stalk may be attached to the cap centrally, off-center, or at the side of the cap. On the underside of the cap there may be **gills,** which are blade-like structures upon which spores are produced. In place of gills, there may be **teeth/spines** or **tubes** (the open end of each tube is called a **pore**). The tubes are packed closely together; their collective pores are known as the **pore surface.** Both teeth/spines and tubes serve the same basic reproductive function as gills. In some species, the underside of the immature cap is covered by a piece of tissue stretching from the cap's edge, or **margin,** to the stalk. This tissue, the **partial veil,** covers and protects the developing gills or tubes. As the mushroom cap expands, the partial veil tears, often leaving remnants on the cap margin or adhering to the stalk, where it forms a **ring.**

Refer to the glossary for more precise definitions of these structures and for other mycological terms that you will encounter in this book.

How to Make a Spore Print

Sometimes key field features alone will not guarantee accurate identification. Spore prints, like finger prints, often bridge the gap between macroscopic and microscopic identification, facilitating more definitive differentiation between otherwise confusing fungi.

Spore prints are formed when the mushroom spores are allowed to drop undisturbed onto a surface. They are simple to make. Cut the cap from the stalk, place it gill-, tooth-, or pore-side down on a piece of clean white paper, and cover it with a cup or dish to prevent disturbance by drafts. Allow eight hours or so for a good, thick spore deposit. You might also wrap one or two mature caps, with fertile surface down, on a piece of white paper while you are collecting in the field. In this way, you might have an adequate spore print ready for your next step in identification once you arrive home.

A spore print is also useful if you intend to do microscopic work, as it is the best source of mature spores.

Collecting and Preserving Dye Mushrooms

Perhaps the most important consideration when collecting mushrooms for dyeing is that proper care be taken to allow one to correctly identify the specimens. This means preserving important field characteristics, recording the habitat and the substrate on

which the mushroom is growing, and noting the tree types that are associated with your collection. Keep specimen collections separate from each other. Wrapping them in waxed paper, or placing them in paper bags is a simple and effective technique.

Unlike collecting mushrooms for consumption, spoilage and insect infestation is not a primary concern. In fact, the best dye results are often obtained from very mature to decaying fungal fruiting bodies (see illustration of *Pholiota malicola*). For example, mature *Sarcodon underwoodii* yield much richer shades of blue and green than young specimens of the same species, and the best tones of orange and pink are obtained from the most decayed, red portions of *Hypomyces lactifluorum*.

Pholiota malicola var. *malicola* (immature)

Pholiota malicola var. *malicola* (mature)

Pholiota malicola var. *malicola* (very mature)

Dye test results of *Pholiota malicola* var. *malicola* (*left to right:* immature, mature, very mature)

Collecting Clothing and Equipment

Basic equipment used for collecting dye mushrooms includes a basket or other rigid container to transport your specimens, a sturdy knife to pry and cut mushrooms free from their substrate, collecting bags or waxed paper to keep collections separate, and a pencil and notebook for recording field notes. Comfortable clothing appropriate to weather and terrain is also strongly recommended.

When to Collect Mushrooms

Mushroom fruiting patterns are affected by numerous conditions including humidity, temperature, daylight length, and precipitation. While it is impossible to predict exactly when mushrooms will fruit, there are some basic guidelines which, if followed, will help ensure a successful foray.

Some species of mushrooms have only one fruiting season, while others have split or multiple fruiting periods. These must be discovered for the particular geographic area in which you are collecting. Generally, the collecting season begins in April and extends through October for most species. Some, like certain polypores, can be collected year-round, even in winter.

Typically, the best time to collect gilled mushrooms and other fleshy fungi is from two to five days after a significant rainfall, or sooner if rains have been falling at frequent intervals. Sunny, windy, dry days may assist with spore dispersal but they reduce fruiting by minimizing the moisture essential to it. Some mushrooms fruit optimally during hot, humid weather, while others prefer cooler temperatures. Late summer and early fall are usually the most abundant seasons for collecting. Of course, there are always exceptions.

Take time to learn weather and fruiting patterns for your own area. Keep notes of when and where you collect species to refer to next year. In this way, you have the best chance of keeping your basket filled.

Where to Collect Mushrooms

Where to collect mushrooms depends on several factors: local weather conditions, the type of mushroom being sought, time of year, and geographic location.

Since most mushrooms require moisture to fruit, during times of extended dry weather the best locations to search for them are in naturally moist areas: in bogs, along the shorelines of ponds and lakes, along the banks of streams, creeks and rivers, and in cool ravines. Fallen trees and stumps often retain moisture longer than the surrounding soil and are good places to explore. However, after several days of rain, these

Hoh Rain Forest

same locations may be too wet and you might do better to search in drier locations: hillsides, meadows and sandy areas.

Because mushrooms require rather specific substrates, and because some exist in a mycorrhizal relationship with specific trees or other plants, the kind of mushroom you are hunting for will affect where you should look: on the ground or on trees, beneath conifers or hardwoods, in meadows, or in bogs. It is extremely helpful to learn what the mushroom requires in order to know where to look for it.

Preserving Dye Mushrooms

There are various techniques, and reasons, for preserving dye mushrooms. Often, it is impossible to collect enough of a particular mushroom type during a single foray, and one must save and add to the collection before having enough for a particular project. Or, one might be lucky enough to find an abundance of good dyers, as can happen with *Phaeolus schweinitzii,* and need to preserve it for later use. Another reason is that dye results vary depending on the age, length, and preservation technique used to save mushrooms. The dye results from fresh specimens can differ drastically from those that are dried. While one may elect to preserve mushrooms by freezing or drying, we recommend drying as the ideal preservation technique. Drying provides optimum consistency in dye results, requires little energy, and allows one to save specimens indefinitely. *All color results reported in this book are from dried mushrooms unless otherwise noted.*

Commercial dehydrators are readily available at most kitchen and gourmet shops, or from food and cooking catalogues. They are relatively inexpensive, use little energy, and are simple to operate. One can also dry mushrooms in an oven set at the lowest temperature setting with the oven door left slightly open, or by threading the mushrooms on a string and hanging them in a dry and well ventilated area. Once dried, mushrooms can be stored in ziplock plastic bags or other air-tight containers. Be sure to label your collections, as some dried specimens are almost impossible to distinguish from others.

Dyeing Equipment

Care should be taken in choosing equipment when mordanting or dyeing wool. Use pots, kettles, measuring cups and spoons that are made from non-reactive materials such as glass, stainless steel, or enamel. Copper, brass, aluminum and iron can affect color results. Other useful items include pH paper, a thermometer, and drying racks for the yarn. Do not store or mix your dyeing equipment with cooking utensils. Some mordants are poisonous, especially tin and chrome. *There is a growing trend among dyers not to use tin and chrome due to their toxicity and their effect on the environment as*

Tending the dye pot

pollutants. Work with them in a well-ventilated area, avoiding inhalation of their fumes. Work outside whenever possible. Do not dispose of solutions containing chrome, copper, or tin in the environment or down the drain into municipal sewage systems. Used solutions containg these mordants should be disposed of at waste collecting sites. Always keep all dyeing chemicals and materials away from children and pets.

Preparing the Wool

Throughout the book we refer to wool as the fiber being dyed. Other natural protein-based animal fibers such as mohair, alpaca, and wool-mohair blends also work well, producing subtle color differences due to the uniqueness of each fiber type. Experiment with silk and silk blends. We do not recommend dyeing cellulose-based fibers such as cotton and rayon, or synthetic fibers such as acrylic. They tend not to take up color well or consistently, and/or they are not colorfast.

Handspun wool is usually spun "in the grease," that is, a good quantity of natural lanolin remains in the wool fiber. For best results, the wool must be **scoured** prior to dyeing. This is a simple process of washing and heating the wool in order to release excess grease and debris. Wool really doesn't mind heat or water. It does mind, and reacts adversely to, sudden extreme changes in temperature and extended periods of boiling. This weakens the fibers and can cause shrinking. If you are using commercially spun wool, it may or may not have been scoured. If you are unsure, it is wise to scour the wool as a precaution. This should also remove any chemical additives that may have been used in processing the wool.

Using a mild detergent, add a few tablespoons to lukewarm water in a large pot or kettle. Add the wool and enough water to cover it completely. Bring the water to approximately 180–195°F (85–90°C)—*do not boil!*—remove from heat, and allow the wool to soak for ½ hour if commercially spun, or 1 hour if handspun. After allowing the wool to cool, squeeze it gently to remove excess water. Do not twist or wring the

Mushroom-dyed silk scarf

yarn. This stretches the fibers and can damage the wool. Finally, rinse the yarn in warm water several times to remove all remaining soap. Soap residue can adversely affect the dyeing process.

At this point, you may continue with the dyeing process or allow the wool to dry for later use.

Mordanting

Chemicals called mordants are often used when dyeing wool in order to **fix** the color, to make it colorfast. Mordants are also used to brighten or **bloom** a color, or to darken or **sadden** a color. When wool is dyed without the addition of mordants, the process is referred to as **substantive dyeing**. When mordants are used, it is known as **adjective dyeing**. The chemicals most commonly used as mordants are: alum (aluminum potassium sulfate), chrome (potassium dichromate), tin (stannous chloride), copper (copper sulfate), iron (ferrous sulfate), cream of tartar (potassium bitartrate), and Glauber's salt (sodium sulfate). Cream of tartar and Glauber's salt are used to brighten, prevent streaking and ensure even distribution of color. Common household ammonia and vinegar are also used to affect color results by changing the pH of the dyebath. For instance, a slightly alkaline dyebath (pH 8–9) obtained by adding a small quantity of ammonia, results in more greens and blues from many *Hydnellum* species and brings out more reds with *Hypomyces lactifluorum* than a neutral dyebath produces (see illus. p. 16).

Wool can be mordanted in one of three ways: before dyeing (premordanting), during dyeing (simultaneous mordanting), and at the end of the dyeing process. Premordanting is perhaps the most common of the three methods. It allows one to mordant large quantities of wool for immediate or later use and provides consistent results. Its disadvantage is that it is the most time consuming method, requiring that

Skeins of unmordanted and mordanted yarn (*left to right:* no mordant, alum, chrome, tin, copper, iron)

Color variations with pH change using *Hypomyces lactifluorum* (*left:* neutral pH; *right:* alkaline pH)

the wool be processed twice: once while premordanting, and again while dyeing. There is also some concern that this double exposure to heat when working with tin or iron might damage the fiber, so care sould be taken to ensure that the wool is not boiled. To premordant wool, dissolve the selected mordant in boiling water and add it to a kettle or pot of warm water, mixing thoroughly. Add yarn that has been tied loosely in skeins and has been presoaked and saturated in warm water for about one-half hour. Heat just to the boiling point, reduce heat, cover, and simmer at approximately 180–195°F (85–90°C) for one hour. Lift and redistribute the yarn often to ensure even absorption and processing. Allow to cool, remove yarn and dry, or continue dyeing. To remove excess water, do not twist or wring the yarn as this can damage the wool; rather, squeeze it gently.

Some people prefer to mordant wool during the dyeing process. This is an especially useful technique when time is critical, or when one is putting on a demonstration for a class or workshop. Known as simultaneous mordanting, one dissolves the selected mordant in boiling water and adds it to the already prepared dyebath. Presoaked wool is added and the whole is heated to approximately 180–195°F (85–90°C) and simmered for one hour. During this time, the wool should be lifted and shifted frequently. Do not stir or mix as this could damage or tangle the yarn. Allow to cool, rinse in warm water, then wash with warm water and soap and rinse again thoroughly.

Saddening and blooming are mordanting techniques used to darken or brighten colors at the end of the dyeing process. The wool is removed from the dyebath after approximately 45 minutes of simmering. A small amout of mordant dissolved in boiling water (iron for saddening, tin for blooming) is added to the dyebath and mixed in. The wool is returned to the dyebath and simmered at 180–195°F (85–90°C) for another 5 to 15 minutes, until the desired color is obtained. Allow to cool, rinse in warm water, wash with warm water and soap, and rinse again thoroughly.

Washing the dyed yarn

The amounts of mordants used for 4 ounces/114 grams of dry wool vary among different sources. Listed below are the most common ranges:

Alum: 1½ teaspoon–5 teaspoons plus 2 teaspoons cream of tartar
Chrome: ¼–½ teaspoon plus 1 teaspoon cream of tartar
Tin: ¼–½ teaspoon plus 4 teaspoons cream of tartar
Copper: 2–3 teaspoons
Iron: 1–4½ teaspoons plus 1 teaspoon cream of tartar, plus 0–6 teaspoons Glauber's salt

Preparing the Dyebath

Once your wool has been prepared and is ready for dyeing, the next step consists of making a "soup" of the dye mushrooms. Typically a 1:1 ratio of wool to dried mushroom weight is used. For example, to dye an ounce of wool, an ounce of dried mushrooms is needed. There are exceptions. Some mushrooms are "good" dyers and produce strong colors. In these cases, fewer mushrooms (less weight) are needed to produce satisfactory dye results. Other mushrooms produce weaker colors and more are needed to obtain the desired color results. *The colors described in this book were obtained by using the 1:1 wool to mushroom weight formula unless otherwise noted.*

Preparing the dye bath

Once you have determined the weight of wool and mushrooms you need to use, break or crush the mushrooms into your dyepot and cover with enough water to allow them to float freely. (*The water you use can influence your color results due to the presence of minerals and/or chemicals.* You might want to experiment, comparing the color results using distilled water with those obtained using your local water). Heat the mushrooms just to boiling, reduce heat, cover and simmer for one hour. Allow to cool, then strain using a fine sieve or cheesecloth in a colander. Squeeze as much liquid as possible from the mushrooms and then discard them, or save for further experimentation. The resulting liquid is known as the **dyebath.** Often the dyebath can be used to dye more than one batch of wool or fiber. After its inital use, the dyebath is known as the **afterbath.** The second use is called the **first afterbath,** the third use is the **second afterbath,** and so on (see illustration of *Hapilopilus nidulans* dyebath results, below). Dyebaths can be saved for future use. Some people freeze them for later use. Aging the dyebath in this way can alter future dye results and may even improve them!

Dye results from successive afterbaths using *Hapalopilus nidulans* (*left to right:* original dyebath, 1st afterbath, 2d afterbath, 3d afterbath)

When dyeing with polypores or tooth fungi, after 10–15 minutes of cooking, add enough household ammonia to bring the pH up to 8–9. This brings out more of the blues and greens. The one exception to this rule is *Phaeolus schweinitzii.* Do not change the pH when dyeing with this mushroom.

Dyeing the Wool

Once you have prepared the dyebath, you are ready to dye your wool. If the wool is dry, allow it to soak in lukewarm water for one-half hour or more. This ensures even and consistent uptake of color. Gently squeeze excess water from the wool, place it into the cooled dyebath, and add enough additional water to allow the wool to "swim" freely in the pot. *It is important not to add cold wool to hot liquid or heated wool to cold liquid. Always avoid extreme temperature changes to prevent damaging the wool fiber.*

Checking for color

Heat just to boiling (180–195°F, 85–90°C), being careful not to boil the wool. Cover and simmer just below boiling for one hour, lifting and shifting the wool frequently to ensure even distribution of color. Allow the wool to cool completely in the dyebath for best results. (If in a hurry, allow to partially cool; remove wool from dyebath and add to successive rinses of water, gradually cooling the wool.) Once cool, rinse the wool until the water runs clear. Wash with a mild soap, rinse thoroughly, and hang until dry. Some people weight their skein of yarn while it is drying. Others remove excess water by spinning the skein on their arm prior to hanging it up to dry.

Swinging skeins to remove excess water

Repeat the steps described above for dyeing successive batches of wool, experimenting with saddening and/or blooming, and pH changes if using polypores or tooth fungi.

The term **colorfast** refers to dyed wool that maintains its color after washing and with exposure to sunlight. Typically, the blue ranges of color obtained from dyeing with mushrooms are not as colorfast as other colors. To determine colorfastness a tester strip of yarn may be dyed, washed, and then exposed to bright sunlight for approximately one week. If a portion of the strip is protected from the sun, it can be used for comparison with the sun-exposed portion to check for possible fading.

Skeins of mushroom-dyed yarn drying on racks

Explanation of the Descriptions of Illustrated Species

Scientific name: A Latin scientific name is provided for each species. The name used may not be the same as is commonly found in other field guides, reflecting a recent taxonomic change. Sometimes an alternative name is listed in the "Comments" section. We have also provided unabbreviated author citations for the convenience of individuals who may find this information useful.

Macroscopic features: The appearance of the fruiting body is described, including size, shape, color, staining reactions, odor and taste. The morphological features of some mushrooms, such as puffballs, are described under the single heading of "Fruiting body." Others have morphological features described under separate headings such as "Cap," "Gills," "Pore surface," and "Stalk." Many mushrooms have distinctive odors; this is noted if useful. The flesh of some species has a distinctive taste and is indicated if known. *If you choose to taste the tissue of a mushroom, be advised that some mushrooms taste hot and peppery and may irritate, burn or numb your mouth if chewed for an extended period.* Note also that there is no significant risk in tasting mushrooms *unless you swallow the tissue!* To safely taste mushrooms, place a small piece in your mouth, chew it for only a few seconds and spit it out. If the taste is mild (not bitter or peppery), wait a minute and then chew a second small piece for 15 to 30 seconds and again spit it out, as some mushrooms' bitter or acrid tastes are subtle.

Spore print: Spore print color is a valuable character for mushroom identification, especially for gilled mushrooms and boletes. It is reliable, usually easy to obtain, and is used as a differentiating character in many of the descriptions.

Microscopic features: Information about spore size, shape, surface features and microscopic color is presented here. Additional information including length of **asci,** shape of **paraphyses,** presence of **setae** and other useful microscopic characters, is included where appropriate.

Macrochemical tests: Color reactions obtained when different chemicals are applied to various parts of the fruiting body are described here.

Fruiting: The **habit** of mushroom growth (solitary, scattered, in groups or clusters), the **substrate, habitat,** fruiting period, frequency, and geographical distribution are described here. The fruiting period is stated as a month-to-month range and describes the time during which the mushroom is likely to occur. On occasion, mushrooms will appear outside of their expected fruiting period due to unusual weather conditions. Frequency is estimated for North America. Species listed as "occasional" may be locally abundant in some areas or rare to absent in others.

Comments: This section includes brief descriptions of similar species, alternate names, explanations, and other useful or interesting information.

Dye notes: Colors obtained from the dyeing process are described here. Results include the colors produced without a mordant, as well as when alum, chrome, tin, copper, or iron have been used. Continuing the method first developed by Miriam Rice, a code of knots is used to denote each mordant as follows:

no mordant	○	no knot
alum	•	one knot
chrome	••	two knots
tin	•••	three knots
copper	••••	four knots
iron	•••••	five knots

While every effort was made to personally test each mushroom described in this book, it was impossible to obtain a sample of each species included. Whenever the **Dye notes** heading is followed by an asterisk (e.g., Dye notes: *), this indicates that the dye results were obtained, and reported, by dyers other than the authors.

Additional information contained in this section includes any pH changes made to obtain the reported colors, specific parts of the mushroom used when applicable, as well as variations in the mushroom to wool ratio described in the section, "Preparing the Dyebath" (page 18).

How to Use the Identification Keys

The mushroom species illustrated in this book are arranged alphabetically in major groups based on similarities in their appearance. The sequence in which these species occur in this book corresponds to the sequence in which they appear in the keys. They are intentionally not arranged by order, family, or genus. Examples of each of the thirteen major groups are illustrated in the Color Key to the Major Groups of Mushrooms. The Color Key and accompanying brief descriptions constitute the foundation upon which this entire work is based.

If you know the identification of a species and wish to read about it, consult the index. If, however, you wish to identify an unknown mushroom, follow the steps presented below. Before attempting the identification procedure, be sure that you have collected as many different stages of growth as possible (in as *fresh* condition as possible), made notes about the habit, habitat, and substrate, and obtained a spore print if one is obtainable. Identifying mushrooms can sometimes be a very difficult task, and every bit of information is useful.

Mushroom Identification Procedure

1. Always start at the beginning of the color key and determine which major group best describes the mushroom you are attempting to identify.
2. Turn to the page indicated for the major group and read the introductory information presented.
3. Examine the color illustrations at the end of the descriptions for the major group and select the one that most closely resembles your unknown specimen. Read the corresponding description and determine whether your choice matches your unknown specimen. Be sure to read the **Comments** section when provided.
4. In the event that you cannot match any description and illustration with your unknown specimen, it is likely that your unknown specimen is not included in this book.

Color Key to the Major Groups of Dye Mushrooms

ALWAYS start at the beginning of the color key and determine which major group best describes the mushroom you are attempting to identify. Turn to the page indicated for the major group and read the introductory information presented. Examine the color photograph(s) at the end of each major group, determine which choice most closely matches your specimen, and read the corresponding description. This key will only identify the major groups that contain dye mushrooms recognized in this work. It is not intended to be, nor should it be used as, a general field guide to the identification of mushrooms. If you already know the identification of a species and wish to read about it, consult the index.

1a Fruiting body with gills, vein-like ridges, teeth (spines), or pores present on the undersurface (if teeth are present, fruiting body *must* have a cap and stalk) → 2.

1b Fruiting body lacking gills, vein-like ridges, teeth (spines), or pores (if teeth are present, fruiting body *must lack* a cap and stalk) → 6.

2a Fruiting body with gills or gill- to vein-like ridges on the undersurface → 3.

2b Fruiting body lacking gills or vein-like ridges → 4.

3a Fruiting body with cap and stalk, or funnel-like shape; undersurface nearly smooth or with blunt, gill- to vein-like ridges which are often forked and crossveined; usually on the ground → **Chanterelles and Allies** (p. 55).

Gomphus clavatus p. 55

3b Fruiting body with cap and stalk, or sometimes stalkless; undersurface with knifeblade-like gills radiating from a stalk or, on stalkless species, from point of attachment to the substrate; growing on a variety of substrates → **Gilled Mushrooms** (p. 65).

Pholiota squarrosa p. 92

Russula ventricosipes p. 94

4a Fruiting body with a cap and stalk and downward oriented spine-like teeth; on the ground → **Tooth Fungi** (illus. p. 115).

Hydnellum aurantiacum p. 117

Hydnellum caeruleum p. 117

4b Fruiting body with pores on the undersurface → 5.

5a Fruiting body fleshy, with cap and typically central stalk; cap undersurface with a sponge-like layer of vertically arranged tubes; the sponge-like layer usually separates easily from the cap tissue; on the ground → **Boletes** (p. 35).

Boletus miniato-olivaceus p. 39

Chalciporus rubinellus p. 45

5b Fruiting body a woody conk, or sometimes fibrous-fleshy to leathery, with pores on its undersurfaces (the pores are sometimes minute; use a hand lens); the pore layer typically does not separate easily from the cap tissue; shape varies from cap-and-stalk to stalkless and shelf-like, or complex clusters; usually on wood → **Polypores** (p. 97).

Fomes fomentarius p. 100

Hapalopilus nidulans p. 103

6a Fruiting body erect, with a conspicuous stalk, or a fan- to vase-shaped cluster with a stalk-like base; interior *never* powdery at maturity → 7.

6b Fruiting body not as above, stalkless or with a short stalk-like base → 10.

7a Fruiting body saddle-shaped or irregularly lobed to cup-shaped with a well developed stalk; on the ground or on decaying wood → **False Morels** (p. 61).

Gyromitra esculenta p. 62

7b Fruiting body not as above → 8.

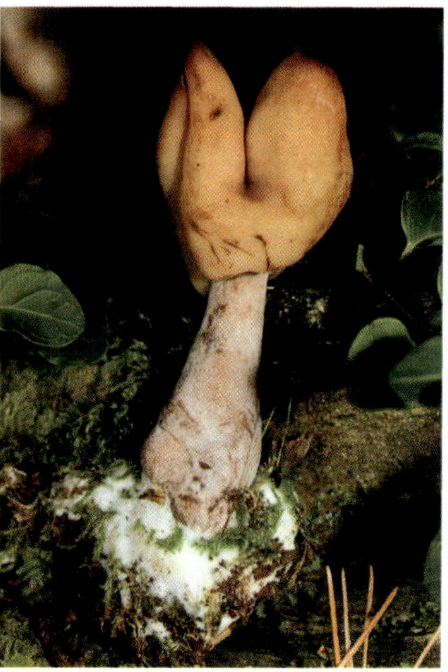

Gyromitra infula p. 62

8a Fruiting body leathery or fibrous-tough, fan- to vase-shaped, often with a split or torn margin; typically some shade of brown at maturity, with or without whitish tips or margins; fertile surface smooth, wrinkled or warty but lacking pores (use a hand lens); on the ground or enveloping roots, branches, seedlings, or mosses → **Fiber Fans and Vases** (p. 63).

Thelephora palmata p. 63

Thelephora vialis p. 64

8b Fruiting body not as above → 9.

9a Fruiting bodies erect, coral-like, repeatedly branched appendages; on the ground → **Coral Fungi** (p. 59).

9b Fruiting body erect, unbranched, resembling tongues or clubs, yellow; on the ground → **Club Fungi** (p. 57).

Ramaria abietina p. 59

Clavariadelphus pistillaris p. 58

Clavariadelphus truncatus p. 58

10a Fruiting body erect and cylindric to club-shaped, or antler-like, surface roughened like sandpaper (use a hand lens), fibrous-tough to woody or hard and carbonaceous, dark gray to black; usually on decaying wood → **Carbon and Cushion Fungi** (p. 54).

Apiosporina morbosa p. 54

Daldinia concentrica p. 54

10b Fruiting body not as above → 11.

11a Fruiting body round to somewhat flattened when young, then splitting into 6–9 star-like rays at maturity; growing on the ground → **Earthstars** (p. 61).

Astraeus pteridis p. 61

11b Fruiting body not as above → 12.

12a Fruiting body round, oval, pear- to turban-shaped, or irregularly rounded, but *not* star-shaped at maturity; usually stalkless but occasionally slightly stalked; growing on the ground or decaying wood, sometimes partially or completely buried → **Puffballs and Allies** (p. 114).

Pisolithus tinctorius p. 114

Scleroderma meridionale p. 114

12b Fruiting body not as above → 13.

13a Fruiting body parasitic, partially or completely covering and usually disfiguring gilled mushrooms; outer surface orange to reddish orange and roughened like sandpaper → **Hypomyces** (p. 96).

Hypomyces lactifluorum p. 96

13b Fruiting body not parasitic; typically hard, thin, spreading, crust-like to leathery and often forming extensive patches; margin sometimes projecting; fertile surface roughened to finely cracked, poroid, folded, or covered with spines → **Crust Fungi** (p. 59).

Phlebia incarnata p. 60

Sarcodontia setosa p. 60

Gymnopilus luteofolius

Dye Mushroom Species
Descriptions & Illustrations

Sarcoscypha austriaca

Descriptions and Illustrations of Dye Mushroom Species

Boletes

Boletes, also known as fleshy pored fungi, are among the most fascinating and highly prized mushrooms. Their beautiful colors, distinctive features, and relative abundance makes them one of the most popular groups collected. Most boletes grow on the ground and are soft and fleshy. They have a cap, stalk, and a sponge-like layer of tubes on the undersurface of the cap. Except for the genus *Gastroboletus,* species of which have enclosed and irregularly arranged tubes, boletes have vertically arranged tubes, each of which terminates in a pore. The tube layer is easily detached and typically separates cleanly from the cap flesh. Polypores also have tubes, but can easily be differentiated from boletes because most grow on wood. Their fruiting bodies are typically tough and leathery to woody, and their tube layers usually do not separate cleanly from the cap flesh.

The majority of boletes are mycorrhizal with trees and only a few can be collected in open fields or grassy areas. One of the most important steps in bolete identification is obtaining a spore print. Although some can be very difficult to identify even with the aid of chemical tests and the microscope, many boletes are easily identified using only macroscopic features.

The best dye results are usually obtained by using primarily the tube layer of boletes. The results described below were obtained in this manner unless otherwise noted.

Boletus aereus Bulliard Illus. p. 130

Cap: 2¾–6" (7–15.5 cm) wide, pulvinate to convex, becoming broadly convex to nearly plane in age, margin even; surface moist or dry, sometimes pitted, glabrous or whitish pruinose, dark brown to blackish brown and often paler toward the margin, sometimes pale reddish brown or mottled with whitish to tan areas; flesh pale vinaceous at first, becoming whitish to pale yellow at maturity, not staining when exposed; odor and taste not distinctive.

Pore surface: white at first, becoming dingy yellow and depressed near the stalk in age; pores angular, 1–3 per mm.

Stalk: 2⅜–4¾" (6–12 cm) long, 1–1½" (2.5–4 cm) thick, nearly equal or enlarged downward, dry, solid, white to pinkish buff at first, becoming pale vinaceous-brown in age, reticulate on the upper half or more; partial veil and ring absent.

Spore print: olive-brown.

Microscopic features: spores 12–14 x 4–5 μm, subfusoid to subellipsoid, smooth, ochraceous.

Macrochemical tests: flesh does not stain with the application of KOH, NH_4OH, or $FeSO_4$.

Fruiting: solitary, scattered or in groups on the ground under hardwoods and mixed woods, especially oak and madrone; September–December; fairly common; California.

Comments: *Boletus edulis* has paler cap colors, often with reddish tones, grows under conifers, and is widely distributed across North America.

Dye notes: *

no mordant	◦	none
alum	·	lemon-yellow
chrome	··	light brown
tin	···	orange
copper	····	olive
iron	·····	olive

Boletus badius Fries

Illus. p. 130

Cap: 1⅛–4" (3–10 cm) wide, pulvinate when young, becoming broadly convex to nearly plane in age, margin even or with a narrow band of sterile tissue; surface dry but slightly viscid when wet or in age, somewhat pruinose at maturity, reddish brown to chestnut-brown or yellow-brown, occasionally olive-tinted in age; flesh whitish when fresh, usually staining yellow then blueing near the tubes when exposed, remainder of the flesh not blueing; odor and taste not distinctive.

Pore surface: pale yellow, becoming greenish yellow and depressed near the stalk in age, staining blue to blue-gray when bruised; pores angular, 1–2 per mm; tubes 8–15 mm deep.

Stalk: 1½–3½" (4–9 cm) long, ⅜–¾" (1–2 cm) thick, equal, solid, dry, slightly pruinose when young, yellowish, becoming predominently brown, reddish brown, tan or colored like the cap, occasionally with a dull rosy tinge, often retaining areas of yellow at the base; partial veil and ring absent.

Spore print: olive-brown.

Microscopic features: spores 10–14 x 4–5 μm, suboblong to slightly ventricose, smooth, yellow.

Macrochemical tests: cap surface stains green to blue with the application of NH_4OH; flesh stains dull blue-green with the application of $FeSO_4$; pore surface stains golden brown with the application of KOH.

Fruiting: solitary or scattered on the ground or on decaying wood, especially conifer, in conifer woods or beech-maple forests; June–November; fairly common; eastern Canada south to North Carolina, west to Minnesota.

Dye notes:

no mordant	◦	yellow
alum	·	yellow
chrome	···	light brownish yellow
tin	···	orange
copper	····	gold
iron	·····	green-brown

Boletus carminiporus A.E. Bessette, Both, and Dunaway Illus. p. 130

Cap: 1⅛–5½" (3–14 cm) wide, convex, becoming broadly convex to nearly plane in age, margin incurved to inrolled at first, becoming decurved at maturity, with a narrow band of sterile tissue; surface dry to subviscid, glabrous or nearly so, dull red at first, becoming pinkish red to orange-red at maturity, fading to reddish orange to dull golden orange in age; flesh whitish to pale yellow, becoming darker yellow when exposed or in age, not blueing at all when exposed; odor and taste not distinctive.

Pore surface: yellow when very young, soon becoming dark red to brownish red, fading to dull red or orange-red in age, staining bluish green then dull olive when bruised, depressed near the stalk at maturity; pores angular to irregular, 2–3 per mm.

Stalk: 2–4½" (5–11.5 cm) long, ⅜–1⅛" (1–3 cm) thick, enlarged downward to a pinched base, rarely tapered downward or nearly equal, dry, solid, distinctly reticulate overall or at least on the upper portion, rose-pink at first, soon becoming dark red at the apex and paler red below, staining brownish red or slowly olive-green to olive-yellow when bruised; flesh pale yellow to yellow, darker than in the cap, unchanging when exposed, becoming dull red around larval tunnels, lacking reddish hairs at the base; partial veil and ring absent.

Spore print: olive-brown.

Microscopic features: spores 8–11 x 3–4 μm, subfusoid, smooth, ochraceous.

Macrochemical tests: cap stains dull golden yellow to pale amber with the application of KOH, olive to yellowish olive with NH_4OH, and olive-gray with $FeSO_4$; flesh stains orange-buff with the application of KOH, bluish gray with NH_4OH, and gray to bluish gray with $FeSO_4$.

Fruiting: solitary, scattered or in groups on the ground in mixed hardwood forests, especially with beech, hickory, and oak, or in mixed woods with oak and pine; June–September; fairly common; southeastern United States from North Carolina south to Florida, west to Arkansas and Louisiana, northern distribution limits yet to be established.

Dye notes:

no mordant	∘	greenish yellow
alum	·	brownish yellow
chrome	··	yellow-brown
tin	···	brownish orange
copper	····	olive
iron	·····	greenish yellow

Boletus edulis Bulliard Illus. p. 130

Cap: 1¾–10" (4.5–25.5 cm) wide, convex to nearly flat; surface smooth to slightly wrinkled, dry, sticky when wet, brown to reddish brown, pale cinnamon-brown, rusty red or yellowish tan; flesh white, not blueing when bruised; odor and taste not distinctive.

Pore surface: white when young, becoming yellow to olive-yellow then brownish yellow to brown in age, staining yellowish olive to dull orange-cinnamon or pale yellowish brown when bruised; pores small, circular, 2–3 per mm.

Stalk: 2–10" (5–25.5 cm) long, ¾–3" (2–7.5 cm) thick, enlarging downward or nearly equal, sometimes bulbous, white or pale brown, with a distinct whitish reticulum on the upper one-third or more, solid; partial veil and ring absent.

Spore print: olive-brown.

Microscopic features: spores 13–19 x 4–6.5 µm, elliptic, smooth, pale yellowish brown.

Fruiting: solitary, scattered or in groups on the ground in woods, especially under conifers; June–February; fairly common; widely distributed across North America.

Comments: This is a complex of many varieties and possibly several species.

Dye notes:

no mordant	∘	greenish yellow
alum	·	gold
chrome	··	brownish yellow
tin	···	dark brownish orange
copper	····	olive
iron	·····	yellowish green

Boletus hypocarycinus Singer

Illus. p. 130

Cap: 1½–3½" (4–9 cm) wide, pulvinate to convex, becoming broadly convex in age, margin typically with a narrow band of sterile tissue, incurved when young; surface dry, tomentose, brown to yellow-brown, sometimes with olive or cinnamon tones; flesh yellow, quickly blueing when cut; odor and taste not distinctive.

Pore surface: red to orange-red or dull orange, quickly blueing when bruised, usually somewhat depressed near the stalk at maturity; pores circular to angular, 2–3 per mm.

Stalk: 2–3¾" (1.5–9.5 cm) long, ⅜–¾" (1–2 cm) thick, nearly equal or slightly enlarged downward, dry, solid, whitish to yellowish with a yellow apex, punctate with carmine-red dots and points at least on the lower portion; flesh yellow, rapidly blueing when cut; mycelium whitish; lacking reticulation, partial veil and ring absent.

Spore print: olive-brown.

Microscopic features: spores 8–12 x 3–4 µm, subfusoid-ellipsoid, smooth, brownish yellow.

Macrochemical tests: cap stains dull golden yellow to pale amber with the application of KOH, olive to yellowish olive with NH_4OH, and olive-gray with $FeSO_4$; flesh stains orange-buff with the application of KOH, bluish gray with NH_4OH, and gray to bluish gray with $FeSO_4$.

Fruiting: solitary, scattered or in groups on the ground or in decaying leaf litter under oaks; June–November; occasional; North Carolina south to Florida, west to Mississippi, distribution limits yet to be established.

Comments: The flesh dries bright yellow. *Boletus luridiformis* is very similar but has larger spores, 12–16 x 4.5–6 µm.

Dye notes:

no mordant	∘	yellowish beige
alum	·	light pinkish brown
chrome	··	light brown
tin	···	gold
copper	····	light brown
iron	·····	beige

Boletus illudens Peck

Illus. p. 130

Cap: 1⅛–3½" (3–9 cm) wide, convex, becoming nearly plane, margin even; surface dry, velvety-subtomentose, pale brownish yellow when young, becoming yellow-brown to pinkish cinnamon; flesh pale yellow, not blueing when cut; odor and taste not distinctive.

Pore surface: lemon-yellow, not blueing when bruised; pores angular, 1–2 mm wide or more on mature specimens.

Stalk: 1⅛–3½" (3–9 cm) long, ¼–½" (5–13 mm) thick, tapered downward, dry, solid, yellow, typically marked with longitudinal rib-like lines that form a partial reticulum; partial veil and ring absent.

Spore print: olive to olive-brown.

Microscopic features: spores 10–14 x 4–5 µm, elliptic to nearly spindle-shaped, smooth, pale brown.

Macrochemical tests: cap surface stains brilliant bluish green, then slowly fuscous with the application of NH_4OH, instantly dark brown with KOH, and slowly stains bluish gray with $FeSO_4$; flesh slowly stains bluish gray with the application of $FeSO_4$.

Fruiting: solitary, scattered or in groups on the ground under oaks in oak or oak-pine woods; July–October; occasional; eastern Canada south to South Carolina, west to Alabama and Minnesota.

Comments: Also known as *Xerocomus illudens. Boletus tenax* has a more tapered stalk with conspicuous coarse reticulation and different macrochemical test reactions.

Dye notes:

no mordant	◦	beige
alum	·	yellow-beige
chrome	··	beige
tin	···	light gold
copper	····	greenish beige
iron	·····	grayish beige

Boletus miniato-olivaceus Frost Illus. p. 27

Cap: 2–6" (5–16 cm) wide, convex, becoming broadly convex to nearly plane in age, margin incurved at first, even or with a narrow band of sterile tissue; surface dry, subglabrous, red to rosy red when extremely young, becoming onion skin-pink to pale rose-pink, sometimes with a bloom, finally becoming rosy tan with olivaceous to yellowish tints or olive-yellow with rosy tints in age; flesh dull white to pale yellow, reddish under the cuticle, blueing when cut, sometimes slowly; odor and taste not distinctive.

Pore surface: yellow at first, becoming dingy olive and sometimes tinted dull reddish in age, depressed near the stalk in age, quickly blueing then slowly staining brown when bruised; pores circular to angular, 1–2 per mm.

Stalk: 2⅜–5" (6–12.5 cm) long, ⅜–¾" (1–2 cm) thick, nearly equal or tapered in either direction, dry, solid, glabrous, yellow overall or with reddish or brownish tinges, especially near the base, not reticulate; partial veil and ring absent.

Spore print: olive-brown.

Microscopic features: spores 10–15 x 4–6 µm, fusoid to subelliptic, smooth, ochraceous; hymenial cystidia vesiculose to utriform.

Macrochemical tests: cap stains olive-yellow then rapidly olive-green to olive-bronze with the application of KOH, orange-yellow to amber-brownish, often with a bluish marginal ring around the stain, with NH_4OH, and grayish olive with $FeSO_4$; flesh stains pale orange with the application of KOH, pale yellowish with $FeSO_4$, and is negative with NH_4OH.

Fruiting: solitary, scattered or in groups on the ground in hardwood forests or mixed woods, usually with beech; June–October; infrequent; eastern Canada south to Florida, west to the Great Lakes region.

Comments: *Boletus sensibilis* is very similar but its cap does not become olivaceous to yellowish in age, its cuticle stains yellow with the additon of KOH or NH_4OH, it has smaller spores, 10–13 x 3.5–4.5 µm, and the odor of its flesh is variously described as faintly fruity, like maple syrup, fenugreek, curry, or licorice.

Dye notes:

no mordant	◦	light yellowish beige
alum	·	yellow
chrome	··	beige
tin	···	light orange
copper	····	brown
iron	·····	light brown

Boletus mirabilis (Murrill) Murrill

Illus. p. 131

Cap: 2–6" (5–15.5 cm) wide, convex, becoming broadly convex to nearly plane in age, margin with a narrow band of sterile tissue; surface dry, velvety-tomentose to appressed-fibrillose or fibrillose-scaly, sometimes areolate in age, maroon to dark red, becoming reddish brown or grayish brown in age; flesh pale yellow, not staining blue when cut or bruised; odor and taste not distinctive.

Pore surface: yellow to greenish yellow, depressed near the stalk at maturity, often staining darker yellow when bruised; pores angular, 1–2 per mm.

Stalk: 3⅛–6" (8–15 cm) long, ⅝–2" (1.6–5 cm) thick, enlarged downward, dry, solid, coarsely reticulate, scurfy, colored like the cap but often paler toward the apex; partial veil and ring absent.

Spore print: olive-brown.

Microscopic features: spores 16–24 x 7–10 µm, elliptical to subfusiform, smooth, yellowish.

Fruiting: solitary or in groups in conifer woods, on or near decaying stumps and logs, especially hemlock; August–November; common in the Pacific Northwest and coastal northern California, west to Michigan where it is uncommon.

Comments: Also known as *Xerocomus mirabilis.* This bolete is frequently attacked by *Hypomyces* species that form powdery white spots on its cap and stalk.

Dye notes: *

no mordant	◦	pale yellow
alum	·	pale yellow
chrome	··	light brown
tin	···	orange
copper	····	olive
iron	·····	olive

Boletus projectellus Murrill

Illus. p. 131

Cap: 1½–8" (4–20 cm) or more wide, convex, becoming broadly convex to nearly plane in age, margin with a narrow band of sterile tissue; surface velvety-subtomentose when young, often rimose in age, dry, pale to dark cinnamon-brown to dull reddish or dark reddish brown, occasionally with gray or olive shades, especially when young; flesh whitish, often with a rosy tinge, not blueing when cut or bruised but slowly changing to yellow-brown; odor not distinctive, taste acidic.

Pore surface: pale yellow to olive-yellow when fresh, becoming brownish olive in age, not blueing but staining lemon-yellow when cut or bruised; pores circular, 0.5–2 mm wide; tubes 1–2.5 cm deep.

Stalk: 3½–9½" (9–24 cm) long, ⅜–2" (1–5 cm) thick, equal or enlarging downward, solid, colored like the cap or somewhat paler, often with a conspicuous white tomentum at the base, with prominent reticulation overall or at least on the upper two-thirds, distinctly viscid at the base in wet weather; partial veil and ring absent.

Spore print color: olive-brown.

Microscopic features: spores 18–33 x 7.5–12 µm, oval to ventricose, smooth, pale brown.

Macrochemical tests: cap surface stains olivaceous with the addition of $FeSO_4$, and is negative for KOH or NH_4OH; flesh stains pale gray with the addition of $FeSO_4$ and is negative for KOH or NH_4OH.

Fruiting: solitary to scattered on the ground under pine; July–September; occasional; eastern Canada south to North Carolina, west to Michigan, and Mexico.

Comments: Also known as *Boletellus projectellus* (Murrill) Singer. This species has the largest spores of any bolete in North America. The sterile projecting margin explains the species name. Compare with *Boletus mirabilis* (Murrill) Murrill, which is primarily a western bolete but has a range overlap with *Boletus projectellus* in the upper Midwest.

Dye notes:

no mordant	∘	yellow
alum	·	yellow
chrome	··	brownish orange
tin	···	dark orange
copper	····	greenish brown
iron	·····	greenish yellow

Boletus rubripes Thiers

Illus. p. 131

Cap: 1½–7" (4–18 cm) wide, convex to pulvinate, becoming broadly convex to nearly plane in age, margin even, incurved to inrolled at first and remaining so well into maturity; surface dry, velvety-tomentose to appressed-fibrillose, often rimose-areolate in age, color variable, buff to olive-buff to olive-brown, staining brown when bruised; flesh whitish to pale yellow, instantly blueing when exposed; odor unpleasant or not distinctive; taste bitter.

Pore surface: yellow at first, becoming olive-yellow at maturity, instantly blueing when bruised, depressed near the stalk in age; pores angular, 1–3 per mm.

Stalk: 2–4¾" (5–12 cm) long, ¾–1¾" (2–4.5 cm) thick, nearly equal or tapered in either direction, dry, solid, glabrous or somewhat longitudinally striate, yellow near the apex and pinkish red to purple-red overall in age, quickly blueing, then slowly staining grayish olive when bruised, mycelium whitish to pale yellow, lacking reticulation; partial veil and ring absent.

Spore print: olive-brown.

Microscopic features: spores 12–18 x 4–5 µm, subfusoid to subcylindric, smooth, ochraceous.

Macrochemical tests: flesh stains yellow-orange with the application of KOH.

Fruiting: solitary, scattered or in groups on the ground in conifer woods or sometimes with oak; July–November; fairly common; Pacific Northwest, Southwest and Mexico, especially common in New Mexico and Colorado.

Dye notes:

no mordant	∘	beige
alum	·	beige
chrome	··	light brown
tin	···	light golden brown
copper	····	light golden brown
iron	·····	light golden brown

Boletus spadiceus Fries Illus. p. 131

Cap: 2–4⅜" (5–11 cm) wide, convex, becoming broadly convex, sometimes nearly plane in age, margin even; surface dry and velvety-subtomentose, sometimes rimose in age, dark olive to olive-yellow with reddish tints, sometimes reddish brown in age; flesh pale yellow with a reddish line beneath the cuticle, initially bright yellow then pinkish around larval tunnels, unchanging or blueing slightly when bruised; odor mild to slightly pungent; taste not distinctive.

Pore surface: yellow to olive-yellow, often but not always staining blue or blue-green when bruised; pores angular, 1–2 mm wide.

Stalk: 1½–4" (4–10 cm) long, ⅜–1" (1–2.5 cm) thick, nearly equal but often narrowed downward, solid, mostly yellow or paler, sometimes with brownish stains but never red, typically whitish and narrowed at the base, often with a yellow basal mycelium, sometimes with raised longitudinal lines forming a partial reticulum at the apex or nearly overall; partial veil and ring absent.

Spore print: olive to pale olive-brown.

Microscopic features: spores 10–14 x 4.5–5 μm, oblong to ventricose, smooth, pale brown.

Macrochemical tests: cap displays a green flash, then stains reddish brown with the application of NH_4OH; flesh stains olive-green with the application of $FeSO_4$.

Fruiting: in groups on the ground in mixed woods and under conifers, along road banks and trails; July–September; infrequent to occasional; eastern Canada south to Pennsylvania, west to Minnesota and California, distribution limits yet to be established.

Dye notes:

no mordant	∘	yellow-beige
alum	·	light bolden brown
chrome	··	yellow-beige
tin	···	gold
copper	····	greenish beige
iron	·····	greenish beige

Boletus speciosus var. *brunneus* Peck Illus. p. 131

Cap: 1½–5½" (4–14 cm) wide, convex, becoming broadly convex to nearly plane in age; surface dry, smooth, lacking scales or conspicuous fibers, reddish brown or yellow-brown to olive-brown; flesh pale yellow, quickly blueing when exposed; odor and taste not distinctive.

Pore surface: bright yellow to yellow when fresh, staining blue when bruised; pores circular to angular, 2–3 per mm.

Stalk: 1½–4¾" (4–12 cm) long, ⅜–1½" (1–4 cm) thick, nearly equal or enlarged downward, solid, yellow on the upper portion, pinkish red to purplish red on the lower portion, or at least tinged reddish, especially near the base, reticulate overall or at least over the upper half, blueing when bruised; partial veil and ring absent.

Spore print: olive-brown.

Microscopic features: spores 10–15 x 3–4 µm, narrowly oblong to subfusoid, smooth, ochraceous.

Macrochemical tests: cap stains amber-orange to orange with the application of KOH or NH_4OH; flesh stains orange with the application of KOH and grayish with $FeSO_4$.

Fruiting: solitary, scattered or in groups on the ground under beech, maples or conifers, especially hemlock; June–September; occasional; eastern Canada south to North Carolina, west to Minnesota.

Dye notes:

no mordant	∘	yellow-beige
alum	·	light yellow-brown
chrome	··	light yellow-brown
tin	···	orange-brown
copper	····	olive
iron	·····	greenish beige

Boletus subvelutipes Peck

Illus. p. 131

Cap: 2⅜–5⅛" (6–13 cm) wide, convex, becoming broadly convex to nearly plane in age, margin even; surface dry, velvety-subtomentose when young, occasionally rimose in age, color variable, cinnamon-brown to yellow-brown, reddish brown, or reddish orange to orange-yellow, quickly staining blue to blue-black when bruised; flesh bright yellow, quickly staining dark blue to blackish when cut or bruised; odor not distinctive; taste mild to slightly acidic.

Pore surface: variable, red, brownish red, dark maroon-red, or red-orange to orange when fresh, often with a yellow rim, duller in age, quickly staining dark blue to blackish when cut or bruised; pores circular, 2 per mm.

Stalk: 1⅛–4" (3–10 cm) long, ⅜–¾" (1–2 cm) thick, nearly equal, solid, furfuraceous, flushed red and yellow, typically yellow at the apex, not reticulate, quickly staining blue to blackish when bruised; often with short, stiff, dark red hairs at the base on mature specimens (immature specimens may have yellow hairs at the base that become dark red in age); partial veil and ring absent.

Spore print: dark olive-brown.

Microscopic features: spores 13–18 x 5–6.5 µm, fusoid-subventricose, smooth, pale brown.

Macrochemical tests: cap stains mahogany-red with the application of KOH or NH_4OH and grayish green to dark olive-green with $FeSO_4$; blued flesh stains rusty orange with the application of KOH or NH_4OH and pale yellow-orange with $FeSO_4$.

Fruiting: solitary to scattered on the ground under hardwoods, especially oak, and conifers, especially hemlock; June–September; fairly common; eastern Canada south to Florida, west to Minnesota.

Dye notes:

no mordant	◦	beige
alum	·	beige
chrome	··	beige
tin	···	light yellow-brown
copper	····	light brown
iron	·····	light brown

Boletus zelleri (Murrill) Murrill

Illus. p. 132

Cap: 2–4" (5–10 cm) wide, convex when young, becoming broadly convex to plane in age, margin even, incurved at first; surface dry, covered with a white bloom and wrinkled when young, becoming subtomentose to smooth at maturity, occasionally slightly areolate in age, with yellow or red tints showing in the cracks, dull black to dark gray to blackish brown, fading to dark brown or dark olive-brown in age, margin often reddish tinged; flesh white to pale yellow, unchanging, or sometimes blueing when exposed; odor and taste not distinctive.

Pore surface: olive-yellow, becoming dark yellow at maturity, often depressed around the stalk in age, typically staining blue when bruised; pores irregular, 1–2 mm wide at maturity.

Stalk: 2–3⅛" (5–8 cm) long, ¼–½" (7–13 mm) thick, nearly equal, dry, solid, longitudinally striate, densely punctate with red to brownish red dots and points over a yellow ground color, the base coated with a white to pale yellow mycelium; partial veil and ring absent.

Spore print: olive-brown.

Microscopic features: spores 12–15 x 4–6 µm, subellipsoid to subventricose, smooth, yellow.

Macrochemical tests: flesh stains greenish with the application of NH_4OH.

Fruiting: solitary, scattered or in groups on the ground or on decaying wood in mixed conifer forests; September–April; common; Pacific Northwest south through California and into Mexico.

Dye notes:

no mordant	◦	yellow
alum	·	yellow
chrome	··	light golden brown
tin	···	orange
copper	····	golden brown
iron	·····	beige

Chalciporus piperatus (Bulliard) Bataille

Illus. p. 132

Cap: ⅝–3½" (1.6–9 cm) wide, convex, becoming nearly plane in age, margin even; surface glabrous or slightly fibrillose, dry or somewhat viscid, sometimes rimose in age, buff to yellow-brown, orange-brown, or reddish brown; flesh pale yellow or tinged reddish, becoming dingy purplish brown in age, not blueing when cut or bruised; odor not distinctive, taste distinctly hot and peppery.

Pore surface: dull cinnamon, reddish cinnamon, or cinnamon-brown, becoming darker reddish brown in age, not blueing when cut or bruised but sometimes staining brown; pores angular, sometimes appearing to radiate from the stalk, 0.5–2 mm wide.

Stalk: 1½–3¾" (4–9.5 cm) long, ¼–½" (6–12 mm) thick, equal or tapered downward, solid, colored like the cap or paler, base with bright yellow mycelium; flesh lemon-yellow, not blueing; partial veil and ring absent.

Spore print: brown to cinnamon-brown.

Microscopic features: spores 9–12 x 4–5 μm, narrowly fusiform, smooth, pale brown.

Macrochemical tests: cap surface stains dark reddish brown with the application of KOH or NH_4OH, and pale grayish green with $FeSO_4$; flesh stains violet-gray with the application of KOH or NH_4OH, and pale grayish green with $FeSO_4$.

Fruiting: solitary, scattered, or in groups on the ground under conifers or hardwoods; July–September; fairly common; widely distributed throughout North America.

Comments: Also known as *Boletus piperatus.*

Dye notes:

no mordant	∘	light brown
alum	·	brown
chrome	··	light brown
tin	···	golden brown
copper	····	light brown
iron	·····	light brown

Chalciporus rubinellus (Peck) Singer

Illus. p. 27

Cap: ¾–1¾" (2–4.5 cm) wide, broadly conic when young, becoming convex in age, margin even; surface dry, viscid when moist, velvety-subtomentose when young, becoming rimose in age, red or reddish when young, yellower in age; flesh bright yellow, not blueing when cut or bruised; odor and taste not distinctive.

Pore surface: bright rose-red when young, becoming dull pink to red in age, not blueing when cut or bruised; pores angular, 1–2 per mm.

Stalk: ¾–1⅜" (2–3.5 cm) long, ¼–½" (6–12 mm) thick, nearly equal, solid, red or reddish initially, sometimes mixed with yellow, not reticulate, lacking yellow mycelium at the base; partial veil and ring absent.

Spore print: brown.

Microscopic features: spores 12–15 x 3–5 μm, subfusoid, smooth, pale dull ochraceous, strongly dextrinoid; pleurocystidia scattered to abundant, 34–62 x 7–12 μm, fusoid-ventricose.

Macrochemical tests: cap surface stains red, then dingy orange with the application of NH_4OH.

Fruiting: solitary, scattered, or in groups on the ground in mixed woods and under conifers; July–September; occasional; eastern Canada south to North Carolina, west to Wisconsin.

Dye notes:

no mordant	∘	golden brown
alum	·	golden brown
chrome	··	golden brown
tin	···	golden brown
copper	····	brown
iron	·····	light brown

The entire mushroom is used.

Fuscoboletinus paluster (Peck) Pomerleau and A. H. Smith Illus. p. 132

Cap: ¾–2¾" (2–7 cm) wide, broadly convex to plane or slightly depressed, with or without an umbo; surface dry, finely tomentose to fibrillose-scaly, pale pinkish purple to reddish purple; margin incurved when young, often appendiculate on immature specimens; flesh yellowish white to yellow, reddish under the cuticle, thin, soft, unchanging when cut; odor not distinctive; taste not distinctive to slightly acidic.

Pore surface: pale yellow when young, becoming golden yellow and finally brownish yellow in age, not blueing when bruised; pores large, angular and radially arranged when young, becoming lamellate and intervenose at maturity, strongly decurrent.

Stalk: ¾–2" (2–5 cm) long, ⅛–5⁄16" (3–7 mm) thick, nearly equal, often rimose, dry, solid, finely pruinose to fibrillose, reticulate to poroid and yellow at the apex, pale pinkish purple to reddish purple below, with a yellow basal mycelium; partial veil reddish purple, fibrillose, very rarely leaving a ring.

Spore print: purple-brown to pinkish brown.

Microscopic features: spores 7–10 x 3–4 μm, elliptical to subelliptical, smooth, pale brown.

Macrochemical tests: cap stains darker purple then bleaches to yellow with the application of NH_4OH.

Fruiting: scattered or in groups, usually among sphagnum mosses, under eastern larch; August–November; occasional; eastern Canada south to Pennsylvania, west to Wisconsin.

Comments: Also known as *Suillus paluster.*

Dye notes:

no mordant	◦	light brownish yellow
alum	·	light golden brown
chrome	··	light golden brown
tin	···	light brownish orange
copper	····	greenish brown
iron	·····	light yellowish brown

The entire mushroom is used.

Gyrodon merulioides (Schweinitz) Singer Illus. p. 132

Cap: 2–4¾" (5–12 cm) wide, convex with an incurved margin when young, soon becoming flat to concave or wavy; surface dry to slightly sticky, smooth or with tiny fibers, yellowish brown to reddish brown, bruising dull yellow-brown; flesh yellow, unchanging or sometimes slowly bruising blue-green when cut; odor and taste not distinctive.

Pore surface: pale yellow to dull gold or olive, decurrent, usually blueing slowly when bruised, gradually discoloring reddish brown; pores elongated and radially arranged, sometimes weakly gill-like, 1 mm or more wide.

Stalk: ¾–1⅝" (2–4 cm) long, ¼–1" (6–25 mm) thick, nearly equal, often curved, off-center, lacking glandular dots, not reticulate, solid, apex colored like the pore surface, lower portion colored like the cap surface, bruising red-brown; partial veil and ring absent.

Spore print: olive-brown.

Microscopic features: spores 7–10 x 6–7.5 μm, oval to nearly round, smooth, pale yellow.

Fruiting: scattered or in groups on the ground, near or under ash trees; July–October; fairly common; eastern Canada south to Alabama, west to Wisconsin.

Comments: also known as *Boletinellus merulioides.*

Dye notes:

no mordant	◦	light brown
alum	·	light brown
chrome	··	light brown
tin	···	dark brownish orange
copper	····	light brown
iron	·····	light brown

The entire mushroom is used.

Gyroporus cyanescens var. *violaceotinctus* Watling

Illus. p. 132

Cap: 1½–4¾" (4–12 cm) wide, convex to broadly convex, occasionally nearly flat; surface dry, coarsely tomentose to floccose-scaly, buff or straw-colored to pale olive, tan to yellowish, often with darker streaks, instantly blueing when bruised; flesh brittle, whitish to pale yellow, instantly staining dark lilaceous to indigo and finally deep blue when cut or bruised; odor and taste not distinctive.

Pore surface: white to yellowish, or pale tan, instantly staining dark lilaceous to indigo when bruised; pores circular, 1–2 per mm.

Stalk: 1½–4" (4–10 cm) long, ⅜–1" (1–2.5 cm) thick, equal or swollen in the middle or below, brittle, stuffed with a soft pith, becoming hollow or developing several cavities in age; surface coarsely tomentose to fibrillose-scaly when young, often smoother in age, not reticulate, colored like the cap or paler, instantly blueing when cut or bruised; partial veil and ring absent.

Spore print: pale yellow.

Microscopic features: spores 8–10 x 5–6 μm, elliptic, smooth, hyaline.

Fruiting: scattered or in groups on sandy soil under birch and maple or in mixed woods; July–September; occasional; widely distributed in eastern North America.

Comments: *Gyroporus cyanescens* var. *cyanescens* is nearly identical, but the flesh stains greenish blue, then blue when cut. It grows in sandy soil in hardwood forests, mixed woods, or along roadcuts.

Dye notes:

no mordant	◦	light yellow
alum	·	light yellow
chrome	··	beige
tin	···	light orange
copper	····	gold
iron	·····	light brownish orange

Phylloporus leucomycelinus Singer

Illus. p. 132

Cap: 1½–3⅛" (4–8 cm) wide, obtuse to convex at first, becoming nearly plane and sometimes shallowly depressed, margin incurved at first, typically with a narrow band of sterile tissue; surface dry, subvelutinous, often rimose to rimose-areolate in age, dark red to reddish brown or chestnut, usually paler on the disc at maturity; flesh whitish to pale yellow; odor and taste not distinctive.

Pore surface: strongly lamellate, decurrent, subdistant to distant, yellow to golden yellow, sometimes forked, strongly intervenose, sometimes poroid near the stalk, not blueing when bruised, separating cleanly from the cap.

Stalk: 1½–3⅛" (4–8 cm) long, ¼–½" (5–13 mm) thick, nearly equal or ventricose at the base, often with distinct ribs near the apex, scurfy or punctate with small reddish brown dots and points, yellow with reddish tinges, with a white to whitish basal mycelium; partial veil and ring absent.

Spore print: yellowish ochraceous.

Microscopic features: spores 8–14 x 3–5 µm, ellipsoid to fusoid, smooth, pale yellowish.

Macrochemical tests: cap surface stains blue with the application of NH_4OH.

Fruiting: scattered or in groups on the ground in hardwood forests under beech and oak; July–October; occasional; eastern Canada south to Florida, west to Michigan.

Comments: Also known as *Phylloporus rhodoxanthus* ssp. *albomycelinus.*

Dye notes:

no mordant	◦	beige
alum	·	beige
chrome	··	beige
tin	···	gold
copper	····	greenish beige
iron	·····	greenish beige

Phylloporus rhodoxanthus Singer

Illus. p. 133

Cap: 1–4" (2.5–10 cm) wide, obtuse to convex at first, becoming nearly plane and sometimes shallowly depressed, margin incurved at first, typically with a narrow band of sterile tissue; surface dry, subvelutinous, often rimose to rimose-areolate in age, color variable, dark red, dull red, reddish yellow to reddish brown or olive-brown; flesh whitish to pale yellow, tinged reddish under the cuticle; odor and taste not distinctive.

Pore surface: strongly lamellate, decurrent, subdistant to distant, bright yellow at first, becoming yellow to golden yellow and finally ochre in age, sometimes forked, strongly intervenose, sometimes poroid near the stalk, not blueing when bruised, separating cleanly from the cap.

Stalk: 1⅛–3½" (3–9 cm) long, ¼–½" (5–13 mm) thick, nearly equal or ventricose at the base, often with distinct ribs near the apex, scurfy or punctate with small reddish brown dots and points, yellow with reddish tinges, with a yellow basal mycelium; partial veil and ring absent.

Spore print: yellowish ochraceous.

Microscopic features: spores 8–14 x 3–5 µm, ellipsoid to fusoid, smooth, pale yellowish.

Macrochemical tests: cap surface stains blue with the application of NH_4OH.

Fruiting: scattered or in groups on the ground in hardwood forests under beech and oak; July–October; occasional; eastern Canada south to Florida, west to California.

Dye notes:

no mordant	◦	beige
alum	·	beige
chrome	··	beige
tin	···	gold
copper	····	greenish beige
iron	·····	greenish beige

Pulveroboletus ravenelii (Berkeley and Curtis) Murrill Illus. p. 133

Cap: ⅜–4" (1–10 cm) wide, bluntly rounded to convex, becoming nearly plane in age, margin incurved when young, typically appendiculate; surface dry and pulverulent at first, becoming appressed-fibrillose to fibrillose-scaly, often slightly wrinkled or rimose in age, bright sulfur-yellow, becoming orange-red to brownish red from the center toward the margin; flesh white to pale yellow, slowly staining pale blue then dingy yellow to pale brown when cut; odor and taste not distinctive.

Pore surface: bright yellow, becoming dingy yellow to grayish brown at maturity, staining greenish blue then grayish brown when bruised; pores angular to nearly circular, 1–3 per mm.

Stalk: 1½–5¾" (4–14.5 cm) long, ¼–⅝" (6–16 mm) thick, equal or enlarging downward, solid, sheathed from the base upward with tiny appressed fibrils, bright sulfur-yellow, bright yellow and smooth above the ring; partial veil membranous and powdery, bright sulfur-yellow, typically leaving a prominent, but sometimes inconspicuous, superior ring.

Spore print: olive-gray to olive-brown.

Microscopic features: spores 8–10.5 x 4–5 μm, elliptic to oval, smooth, pale brown.

Fruiting: solitary, scattered, or in groups on the ground in woods; July–October; occasional to fairly common; widely distributed from eastern Canada south to the Gulf of Mexico, west to Texas, Michigan, and California.

Comments: This distinctive and unique bolete is named for H. W. Ravenel, a nineteenth-century mycologist who worked in South Carolina and Texas.

Dye notes: *

no mordant	∘	yellow
alum	·	gold
chrome	··	greenish yellow
tin	···	orange
copper	····	greenish yellow
iron	·····	olive

Suillus americanus (Peck) Snell Illus. p. 133

Cap: 1⅛–4" (3–10 cm) wide, rounded with an incurved margin when young, becoming broadly convex in age, occasionally with an umbo; surface viscid to glutinous when moist, bright yellow to ochre-yellow, with cinnamon to reddish patches or streaks, margin appendiculate with white to yellow or pale brown cottony veil tissue; flesh yellow, staining purplish brown when cut; odor and taste not distinctive.

Pore surface: yellow when young, slightly browner in age, slowly staining reddish brown when cut or bruised; pores angular, occasionally radially elongated, often decurrent, 1–2 mm wide.

Stalk: 1⅛–3½" (3–9 cm) long, ⅛–⅜" (3–10 mm) thick, nearly equal, becoming hollow, often crooked, not reticulate, yellow, speckled with reddish to dark brown glandular dots and smears, often developing wine-red or wine-brown stains when bruised or in age; veil present, covering most or all of the pore surface when young, but typically remaining attached to the edge of the cap and not leaving a ring on the stalk.

Spore print: brown.

Microscopic features: spores 8–11 x 3–4 μm, nearly fusiform, smooth, pale brown.

Macrochemical tests: cap displays a pink flash, then stains red and finally black with the application of NH_4OH, and stains black with KOH; flesh stains olive with the application of $FeSO_4$.

Fruiting: solitary, in groups or in clusters on the ground under white pine; July–October; fairly common to common; eastern Canada south to North Carolina, west to Minnesota, also recorded from the southwestern United States.

Dye notes:

no mordant	∘	beige
alum	·	light brown
chrome	··	light brown
tin	···	reddish brown
copper	····	light greenish brown
iron	·····	grayish beige

The entire mushroom is used.

Suillus cothurnatus Singer

Illus. p. 133

Cap: ⅝–2⅜" (1.6–6 cm) wide, obtuse to convex, becoming broadly convex, sometimes with a low umbo, margin incurved at first, typically appendiculate; surface smooth, glabrous, viscid, color variable, yellow to orange-yellow, yellow-brown, cinnamon, olive-brown to grayish brown or dark brown; flesh marbled orange-buff and pale yellow, staining dark purple-drab; odor fragrant or not distinctive; taste not distinctive.

Pore surface: pale yellow to orange-yellow, brownish yellow in age, unchanging when bruised; pores irregular to radially elongate, 1–2 per mm.

Stalk: 1–2⅜" (2.5–6 cm) long, 3⁄16–⅜" (5–10 mm) thick, nearly equal or tapered downward, dry, solid, whitish to yellowish, often brownish at maturity, with brownish glandular dots; partial veil fairly thick, baggy, whitish, slightly rubbery, glutinous on the outer layer, typically lacking a conspicuously thickened cottony roll at the base, forming a band-like ring, often with the lower edge flaring; basal mycelium salmon-colored.

Spore print: brown.

Microscopic features: spores 8–10 x 2.5–3.5 μm, ellipsoid-oblong to subcylindric, smooth, honey-brown.

Macrochemical tests: cap stains brown with the application of KOH.

Fruiting: scattered or in groups in sandy soil or on mossy trunks near or under pine; May–October; occasional to locally common; Texas east to Florida, north to North Carolina, limits uncertain because of confusion with *Suillus salmonicolor* (Frost) Halling.

Comments: *Suillus salmonicolor* is nearly identical but has a thicker, more rubbery veil that often has a conspicuously thickened cottony roll at the base and differs microscopically.

Dye notes:

no mordant	∘	beige
alum	·	light brown
chrome	··	light brown
tin	···	brownish orange
copper	····	light brown
iron	·····	beige

Suillus granulatus (Linnaeus) Kuntze Illus. p. 133

Cap: 2–4¾" (5–12 cm) wide, broadly convex, margin of both young and mature caps even; surface viscid to glutinous and often streaked or checkered when fresh, color variable, pale yellow or some shade of tan, brown, cinnamon, or orangish cinnamon; flesh white to pale yellow, not staining blue when cut or bruised; odor and taste not distinctive.

Pore surface: whitish to pinkish buff when young, soon becoming yellowish, staining dull cinnamon in age or when bruised, sometimes unchanging; pores irregular, 1 per mm.

Stalk: 1⅝–3⅛" (4–8 cm) long, ⅜–1" (1–2.5 cm) thick, nearly equal, solid, whitish when young, becoming yellowish in age, especially at the apex, with conspicuous pinkish tan to brownish glandular dots and smears; partial veil and ring absent.

Spore print: brown.

Microscopic features: spores 7–10 x 2.5–3.5 μm, oblong or tapered slightly to the apex, pale brown.

Macrochemical tests: cap stains dark olive to olive-gray with the application of KOH and bluish gray with NH_4OH or $FeSO_4$; flesh stains olive-gray with the application of $FeSO_4$, pink, then pinkish brown with KOH, and pinkish orange, then bluish to purplish with an orange border with NH_4OH; stalk stains purplish brown with the application of KOH or NH_4OH and dark green with $FeSO_4$; pore surface instantly stains rusty orange then rapidly purplish brown with the application of KOH, rusty orange with NH_4OH, and olive-green with $FeSO_4$.

Fruiting: scattered or in groups on the ground under pines; June–November; common; eastern Canada south to South Carolina, west to California and the Pacific Northwest.

Dye notes:

no mordant	∘	beige
alum	·	beige
chrome	··	light brown
tin	···	brownish orange
copper	····	brown
iron	·····	light brown

The entire mushroom is used.

Suillus grevillei (Klotzch) Singer Illus. p. 133

Cap: 1⅜–5½" (3.5–14 cm) wide, convex, becoming broadly convex to nearly plane in age, margin incurved at first, appendiculate; surface glabrous, shiny, viscid to glutinous, color variable, orange-yellow, dull red, red-brown, reddish brown, dark reddish brown or dark chestnut-brown; flesh pale orange-yellow, bruising pinkish brown; odor not distinctive or acid-metallic; taste not distinctive.

Pore surface: yellow when young, darkening to olive-yellow or olive-brown in age, staining brownish when bruised, adnate to depressed; pores angular, 1–3 per mm.

Stalk: 1½–5½" (4–14 cm) long, ⅜–1⅛" (1–3 cm) thick, nearly equal or enlarging slightly downward, solid, yellow and smooth above the ring, streaked reddish brown to brown below and often whitish near the base, glutinous to viscid; partial veil yellowish with reddish brown streaks, cottony with a gelatinous covering, forming a gelatinous superior ring; lacking glandular dots; flesh yellowish, occasionally staining bright green, especially near the base when cut.

Spore print: dull cinnamon-brown.

Microscopic features: spores 8–10 x 2.5–4.5 µm, ellipsoid, smooth, pale straw to nearly hyaline.

Macrochemical tests: cap stains dark green to olive-black with the application of NH_4OH, and greenish black with KOH; flesh stains olive-brown to olive-black with the application of $FeSO_4$, red to pinkish then blue to blue-green with NH_4OH, and displays a pink flash that immediately becomes blue to bluish black with KOH.

Fruiting: scattered or in groups on the ground or among sphagnum mosses under larch; September–November; fairly common; northeastern North America, west to the Pacific Northwest and Alaska.

Comments: Some authors consider the darker colored form to be either a variety, *Suillus grevillei* var. *clintonianus,* or a distinct species, *Suillus clintonianus.*

Dye notes:

		Lighter colored form		*Darker colored form*
no mordant	∘	none	∘	light beige
alum	·	beige	·	light golden brown
chrome	··	grayish beige	··	light brown
tin	···	light gold	···	light gold
copper	····	greenish brown	····	brown
iron	·····	light brown	·····	gray

Tylopilus alboater (Schweinitz) Murrill

Illus. p. 134

Cap: 1⅛–5⅞" (3–15 cm) wide, convex, becoming broadly convex to nearly plane in age, margin often with a narrow band of sterile tissue; surface dry, velvety-tomentose, occasionally finely rimose in age, black to dark grayish brown, often covered with a thin whitish bloom when young; flesh white or tinged gray, staining pinkish to reddish gray when cut or bruised, eventually blackening; odor and taste not distinctive.

Pore surface: white or with a tinge of gray when young, becoming dull pinkish or flesh-colored in age, not dark gray or black, usually staining reddish then slowly black when bruised; pores angular to irregular, about 2 per mm.

Stalk: 1½–4" (4–10 cm) long, ⅝–1½" (2–4 cm) thick, equal or enlarging downward, solid, colored like the cap or paler, especially near the apex, often covered with a thin whitish bloom, not reticulate or only slightly so at the apex; partial veil and ring absent.

Spore print: pinkish to deep flesh-color.

Microscopic features: spores 7–11 x 3.5–5 µm, narrowly oval, smooth, hyaline.

Macrochemical tests: cap stains amber-orange with the application of KOH and is negative with NH_4OH or $FeSO_4$; flesh stains pinkish orange with the application of KOH, olive, then brownish orange with NH_4OH, and instantly grayish blue to greenish blue with $FeSO_4$.

Fruiting: solitary to scattered on the ground under hardwoods, especially oak; June–September; occasional or locally common; New England south to Florida, west to Missouri, and Mexico.

Comments: *Tylopilus atronicotianus* is very similar but its cap is olive-brown to grayish brown and glabrous or nearly so.

Dye notes:

no mordant	∘	beige
alum	·	greenish brown
chrome	··	greenish brown
tin	···	greenish brown
copper	····	dark greenish brown
iron	·····	pinkish brown

Tylopilus atronicotianus Both

Illus. p. 134

Cap: 3–8" (7.5–20 cm) wide, hemispheric, becoming broadly convex to nearly plane in age, margin strongly inrolled when young, becoming decurved, with a narrow band of sterile tissue; surface dry glabrous or nearly so, somewhat shiny, olive-brown to pale olive-brown or bronze-brown, sometimes grayish brown, rarely pale brownish, darker in age; flesh whitish, slowly staining pink to pinkish red or reddish vinaceous then blackish when exposed; odor musty or not distinctive; taste not distinctive.

Pore surface: white at first and remaining so for some time, slowly becoming vinaceous-cinnamon to pale reddish brown, cocoa-brown to dark reddish brown and depressed near the stalk in age; pores angular to irregular, up to 1.5 mm wide; tubes 8–22 mm deep, bright brown, staining blackish when cut.

Stalk: 2⅜–4¾" (6–12 cm) long, ⅝–1¾" (1.5–4.5 cm) thick, tapered in either direction, sometimes nearly equal or subbulbous, usually with a whitish pointed root-like base, dry, solid, delicately blackish tomentose and pruinose, whitish at the apex, vinaceous-gray to fuscous or dark brown below, becoming blackish near the base, lacking reticulation or only finely so at the apex; flesh grayish to blackish; partial veil and ring absent.

Spore print: reddish brown to cocoa-brown.

Microscopic features: spores 7.5–10.5 x 4–5 μm, narrowly oval, smooth, hyaline.

Macrochemical tests: cap surface stains blackish brown to reddish black with the application of NH_4OH, and reddish brown to brown with KOH; flesh stains pale grayish yellow surrounded by black with the application of NH_4OH, and reddish orange to bright orange-amber or amber-brown surrounded by a black ring with KOH.

Fruiting: solitary, scattered or in groups on the ground in mixed stands of red oak, beech and hemlock, apparently associated with oak; July–September; fairly common; recorded only from western New York, distribution limits yet to be established.

Comments: The name *atronicotianus* means dark tobacco, a reference to the color of the cap. *Tylopilus alboater* is very similar but its cap is black and velvety-tomentose.

Dye notes:

no mordant	∘	beige
alum	·	light brown
chrome	··	light brown
tin	···	greenish brown
copper	····	light grayish brown
iron	·····	pinkish brown

Carbon and Cushion Fungi

Members of this group belong to the class Pyrenomycetes, commonly called the Flask Fungi. Their fertile surfaces are finely roughened like sandpaper, due to the protruding necks of numerous flask-shaped reproductive structures called perithecia, which produce ascospores. They occur on decaying wood (usually hardwood) and sometimes on the surrounding ground. Most species in this group are fibrous-tough to woody, and several are hard, black, and carbonaceous. Some resemble Crust Fungi but differ by having a finely roughened, sandpaper-like surface.

Apiosporina morbosa (Schweinitz) van Arx Illus. p. 30

Fruiting body: 1⅜–5½" (3.5–14 cm) long, ⅜–1" (1–2.5 cm) thick, spindle-shaped to clavate or irregular elongated swellings; surface hard, black, carbonaceous, finely roughened, typically furrowed, and cracked; stalk absent; flesh white when very young, soon black and brittle; perithecia embedded near the surface in a single layer.

Microscopic features: spores 14–22 x 3–6 µm, narrowly elliptic, 1–3 septate, smooth, pale yellowish brown.

Fruiting: solitary or several, clasping and enveloping branches and twigs of cherry and plum trees; year-round; very common; widely distributed in North America wherever its hosts are found.

Comments: It is also known as *Dibotryon morbosum*. This fungus is a widely distributed and highly destructive pathogen of cherry and plum trees.

Dye notes:

no mordant	∘	grayish beige
alum	·	light brown
chrome	··	light greenish brown
tin	···	light greenish brown
copper	····	light brown
iron	·····	gray

Daldinia concentrica (Bolton : Fries) Cesati and de Notaris Illus. p. 30

Fruiting body: ¾–2" (2–5 cm) wide, cushion-shaped to nearly round or irregular; surface uneven and furrowed, reddish brown, becoming black, somewhat shiny, finely roughened, often with minute pores; flesh concentrically zoned when cut vertically, fibrous to powdery and carbon-like, dark purplish brown alternating with darker or sometimes whitish zones; perithecia embedded in a single layer near the surface.

Microscopic features: spores 12–17 x 6–9 µm, irregularly elliptic with one side flattened, smooth, dark brown.

Fruiting: solitary or in clusters on decaying hardwood trees; year-round; common; eastern North America and the Pacific Northwest.

Dye notes:

no mordant	∘	brown
alum	·	brown
chrome	··	brown
tin	···	brown

copper	....	dark brown
iron	.....	brown

The colors reported above were obtained using fresh specimens. Old, dry speciemens produce little or no color.

Daldinia grandis Child Illus. p. 134

Fruiting body: ⅜–2" (1–5 cm) wide, flattened-hemispherical or sometimes irregular; surface uneven, roughened, sometimes furrowed, dark vinaceous-brown when young, becoming black at maturity, dull or somewhat shiny, often with minute pores; flesh dry, usually concentrically zoned, often somewhat shiny, brittle, fibrous to powdery and carbon-like, dark brown to grayish black; perithecia embedded in a single layer near the surface.

Microscopic features: spores 14–26 x 6–11 μm, elliptical to elongated with bluntly rounded ends, smooth, dark brown.

Fruiting: solitary or in groups or clusters on decaying hardwood trees, especially oak; year-round; common; Minnesota west to Washington, south to Arizona and California.

Dye notes:

no mordant	○	brownish green
alum	.	brownish green
chrome	..	grayish green
tin	...	brownish green
copper	....	brownish green
iron	.....	brown

The colors reported above were obtained using fresh specimens. Old, dry specimens produce little or no color.

Chanterelles and Allies

Members of this small group produce fruiting bodies that are often funnel- to vase-shaped at maturity. Many resemble gilled mushrooms but their spores are not produced on true gills. Their fertile surfaces are typically blunt, gill- to vein-like ridges that are often forked or joined together by crossveins, and a few have nearly smooth fertile surfaces.

Gomphus clavatus (Fries) S.F. Gray Illus. p. 134

Cap: 1⅛–4" (3–10 cm) wide, cylindric, and truncate with a depressed center when young, becoming funnel-shaped to somewhat flattened in age, often perforated at the center; surface smooth, lacking prominent scales, violet when young, becoming tan to brownish yellow in age; margin uplifted, wavy, often lobed at maturity.

Flesh: thick, soft, brittle to fibrous, whitish to pale buff; odor and taste not distinctive.

Fertile surface: decurrent, with blunt, vein-like ridges and crossveins, violet to grayish violet, becoming dull ochre to tan in age.

Stalk: up to 2" (5 cm) long below the fertile surface, up to ¾" (2 cm) thick at the apex, tapering downward, often fused with adjacent stalks, solid, colored like the fertile surface.

Spore print: ochraceous.

Microscopic features: spores 10–13 x 4–6.5 µm, narrowly elliptic to spindle-shaped, minutely warted, hyaline.

Fruiting: scattered, in groups or clusters on the ground under conifers; August–October; infrequent to rare; eastern Canada, south to North Carolina, west to the Pacific Northwest, south to California.

Dye notes: *

no mordant	∘	none
alum	·	none
chrome	··	none
tin	···	none
copper	····	none
iron	·····	grayish purple

Polyozellus multiplex (Underwood) Murrill

Illus. p. 134

Fruiting body: ¾–4" (2–10 cm) wide, 2⅜–6" (6–15.5 cm) tall, composed of clusters of vase-shaped to fan-shaped, depressed caps with wavy edges; upper surface dry to moist, grayish purple or bluish gray to dark gray, becoming blackish in age.

Flesh: thick, soft, grayish purple; odor aromatic; taste not distinctive.

Fertile surface: decurrent, with blunt vein-like ridges, grayish purple, often coated with a whitish bloom.

Stalk: ¾–2" (2–5 cm) long below the fertile surface, ⅜–1" (1–2.5 cm) thick, tapered downward to somewhat irregular, dry, solid, grayish purple to dark brown, becoming blackish in age, typically fused with other stalks near the point of attachment.

Spore print: white.

Microscopic features: spores 6–8.5 x 5–8 µm, globose to broadly elliptical, angular, and warted, hyaline.

Fruiting: clustered on the ground in conifer woods; June–October; occasional; throughout northern North America and the Rocky Mountains.

Dye notes:

no mordant	∘	moss-green
alum	·	dark blue-gray
chrome	··	dark gray-green
tin	···	dark blue-gray
copper	····	dark moss-green
iron	·····	dark gray

Club Fungi

Members of this group form erect fruiting bodies that resemble clubs. They lack a cap or head and consist of a club-shaped to cylindric stalk.

Clavariadelphus ligula Fries

Illus. p. 134

Fruiting body: ¾–3¾" (2–9.5 cm) high, ⅛–⅝" (3–16 mm) wide, cylindric to clavate or sometimes irregularly flattened to spoon-shaped, smooth to somewhat wrinkled, pale ochraceous-buff to pale salmon, or vinaceous-buff; apex somewhat pointed or blunt; base white tomentose to strigose with abundant white mycelium binding to the substrate; flesh firm or spongy, white, not staining when bruised; odor not distinctive; taste not distinctive or slightly bitter to metallic; stalk poorly defined, whitish.

Spore print: white.

Microscopic features: spores 10–17 x 3–6 μm, narrowly ellipsoid, smooth, hyaline with yellow oil drops or granular content.

Fruiting: scattered or in dense groups on conifer debris; July–November; fairly common; eastern Canada south to New England, west to the Pacific Northwest and California.

Dye notes:

no mordant	◦	light beige
alum	·	beige
chrome	··	light green
tin	···	light golden brown
copper	····	light golden brown
iron	·····	grayish purple

Clavariadelphus occidentalis Methven

Illus. p. 134

Fruiting body: 2–8" (5–20 cm) high, ⅜–1⅛" (10–30 mm) wide, somewhat spindle-shaped at first, becoming clavate and laterally compressed in age, unbranched, smooth to longitudinally wrinkled, apex usually rounded and sometimes inflated, pale yellow to orange-white when young, becoming grayish orange in age, base pale yellow to whitish, slowly staining brownish when handled or bruised; flesh thick, firm, becoming soft and spongy, whitish, slowly staining brown on exposure; odor and taste not distinctive; stalk poorly defined, whitish.

Spore print: white.

Microscopic features: spores 9.5–13 x 5.5–7 μm, broadly ovate to almond-shaped, smooth, pale yellow with oil drops.

Fruiting: scattered or in groups, or sometimes in clusters on the ground in conifer or mixed conifer and hardwoods; December–February; occasional; Alaska, Arizona, California, Idaho.

Comments: Compare with *Clavaridelphus pistillaris,* which has a darker fruiting body, usually grows in hardwood forests, and has somewhat larger spores.

Dye notes:

no mordant	◦	none
alum	·	none
chrome	··	light bluish gray
tin	···	light beige
copper	····	golden brown
iron	·····	dark purple

Clavariadelphus pistillaris (Fries) Donk

Illus. p. 29

Fruiting body: 2¾–8" (7–20.5 cm) high, ⅜–1¾" (1–4.5 cm) wide, cylindric when young, becoming club-shaped with age, unbranched or rarely forked, smooth to longitudinally wrinkled, apex usually rounded and inflated, yellowish to orange-yellow, becoming brownish orange to pale reddish brown at maturity, slowly staining brownish when bruised; flesh thick, firm or spongy, white, staining brownish when cut; odor not distinctive; taste mild to bitter; stalk poorly defined, white.

Spore print: white to creamy white.

Microscopic features: spores 10.5–14 x 6–7.5 µm, elliptic, smooth, hyaline with yellow oil drops.

Fruiting: scattered or in groups on the ground, usually in hardwoods; July–May; occasional; eastern North America and the West Coast.

Comments: Compare with *Clavariadelphus occidentalis,* which has a paler fruiting body, grows in conifer or mixed woods, and has somewhat smaller spores.

Dye notes:

no mordant	◦	none
alum	·	beige
chrome	··	beige
tin	···	light yellow
copper	····	light green
iron	·····	grayish purple

Clavariadelphus truncatus (Quélet) Donk

Illus. p. 29

Fruiting body: 2–6" (5–15.5 cm) high, 1–2¾" (2.5–7 cm) wide, club-shaped to top-shaped, narrowing downward; typically unbranched but sometimes forking, smooth near the base, becoming longitudinally wrinkled upward; apex flattened and often slightly depressed; golden yellow to orange-yellow or pale brownish orange, usually darkest toward the base; flesh thick, firm or spongy, white; odor not distinctive; taste sweet or bland; stalk poorly defined, white, often with a dense, white, basal mycelium imbedded in the substrate.

Spore print: pale brownish yellow.

Microscopic features: spores 9–12 x 5–8 µm, broadly elliptic, smooth, hyaline with yellow oil drops.

Fruiting: scattered or in groups on the ground in conifer woods; August–October; occasional; widely distributed in North America.

Dye notes:

no mordant	◦	none
alum	·	beige
chrome	··	beige
tin	···	beige
copper	····	greenish beige
iron	·····	grayish purple

Coral Fungi

Coral fungi are species with erect, repeatedly branched, coral-like stalks, which grow solitary or in groups. Most species have brittle flesh and are easily broken, but some are fibrous to tough and flexible. Spores are produced on portions of the smooth to wrinkled outer surface of the stalks and branches. While most species grow on the ground, some occur on decaying wood or on the bark of standing trees.

Ramaria abietina Quélet

Illus. p. 29

Fruiting body: 1⅛–4" (3–10 cm) high and wide, coral-like, arising from a slender stalk; stalk up to 1⅛" (3 cm) long, up to ½" (1.3 cm) thick, dry, solid, white to ochraceous or colored like the branches, with white rhizomorphs at the base; branches repeatedly divided, pliant, ochraceous to cinnamon-buff when young, becoming olive-brown to pale cinnamon with green stains, especially toward the base, in age or in cold weather; branch tips pointed, paler than the branches, sometimes with green stains; flesh spongy, white; odor not distinctive; taste bitter or not distinctive.

Spore print: pale yellowish tan.

Microscopic features: spores 5–8 x 3–5 µm, elliptic, minutely echinulate, hyaline.

Fruiting: solitary, scattered or in groups on the ground under conifers or sometimes hardwoods; August–March; northern North America and the West Coast, especially California.

Comments: Also known as *Ramaria ochraceovirens.*

Dye notes:

no mordant	∘	beige
alum	·	beige
chrome	··	beige
tin	···	yellow-beige
copper	····	greenish beige
iron	·····	gray

Crust Fungi

This is a very large and highly variable complex of species that form thin spreading crust-like to papery growths, usually on decaying wood. Some species are nearly flat, while others have small, projecting, shelf-like caps usually formed by bending backward at the margin. Their fertile surfaces may be rough, warted, wrinkled, cracked, tooth-like or smooth, but lack true pores and are not finely roughened like sandpaper. Crust-like species with pores on their fertile surfaces are included in the Polypores.

Cystostereum murraii (Berkeley and Curtis) Pouzar

Illus. p. 135

Fruiting body: ¾–4" (2–10 cm) wide, thin, crust-like, becoming confluent and spreading to form patches 8" (20 cm) or more in diameter; fertile surface whitish to grayish or pale yellow to pale tan, uneven, roughened and finely cracked, dull; margin on the upper side bent backward forming a dark brownish black shelf with irregular concentric ridges and radial folds, sometimes covered with moss, projecting ⅛–⅜" (3–10 mm).

Spore Print: white.

Microscopic features: spores 4–5 x 2–2.5 µm, oval and flattened on one side to nearly elliptic, smooth, hyaline.

Fruiting: on logs of hardwoods, especially beech; April–October; fairly common; eastern Canada south to North Carolina, west to Minnesota and Missouri.

Comments: formerly known as *Stereum tuberculosum* and *Stereum murraii.*

Dye notes:

no mordant	∘	beige
alum	·	beige
chrome	··	pinkish beige
tin	···	beige
copper	····	beige
iron	·····	dark brownish pink

Phlebia incarnata (Schrader : Fries) Nakasone and Burdsall

Illus. p. 31

Fruiting body: ¾–1⅝" (2–4 cm) wide, 1⅛–3⅛" (3–8 cm) long, fan-shaped to semicircular, stalkless, leathery; sterile (upper) surface moist or dry, finely pubescent to subglabrous, coral-pink when young and fresh, becoming salmon-buff in age; fertile (lower) surface poroid, consisting of a network of radiating, branched folds, pinkish ochre to salmon-buff.

Flesh: about ⅛" (2–4 mm) thick, spongy to leathery, whitish to buff.

Spore print: white.

Microscopic features: spores 4–5 x 2–3 µm, elliptic, smooth, hyaline.

Fruiting: in overlapping clusters on logs and stumps of hardwoods; August–October; occasional; New England west to Missouri, south to Florida and Texas.

Comments: Also known as *Merulius incarnatus. Phlebia tremellosa* = *Merulius tremellosus* has a hairy to wooly, white to pale yellow upper surface, a yellowish to brownish orange or pinkish orange fertile surface, and spores that measure 3–4 x 0.5–1.2 µm.

Dye notes:

no mordant	∘	pinkish beige
alum	·	gold
chrome	··	golden brown
tin	···	pinkish biege
copper	····	pinkish brown
iron	·····	gray-brown

Sarcodontia setosa (Persoon) Donk

Illus. p. 31

Fruiting body: 2–10" (5–25 cm) wide, resupinate, thin, spreading patches that are tightly attached to the substrate; fertile surface consisting of densely crowded, waxy, pale to bright yellow, downward pointed spines that measure up to ½" (1.2 cm) long and often develop reddish stains; flesh thin, waxy; odor sickeningly sweet and unpleasant; taste fruity or not distinctive.

Spore print: white.

Microscopic features: spores 5–6 x 3–4 µm, lacrymoid, smooth, hyaline, thick-walled, with one or more oil drops.

Fruiting: on trunks, logs, and branches of damaged or decaying fruit trees, especially apple, rarely on other hardwoods; July–November; uncommon; widely distributed in North America

Dye notes:

no mordant	∘	pinkish brown
alum	·	pinkish brown
chrome	··	pinkish brown
tin	···	pinkish brown
copper	····	pinkish brown
iron	·····	pinkish brown

Earthstars

The fruiting bodies of earthstars are round to somewhat flattened when young and split into 6–9 star-like rays at maturity. They lack a stalk and grow on the ground.

Astraeus pteridis (Shear) Zeller

Illus. p. 30

Fruiting body: 3⅛–6" (8–16 cm) wide when fully expanded, round to somewhat flattened when young, then splitting into 6–9 rays.

Rays: ⅛–¼" (3–6 mm) thick, fibrous-tough, hygroscopic, inner surface typically conspicuously cracked in a checkered pattern, yellowish tan with dark brown in the cracks.

Spore case: ¾–2" (2–5 cm) wide, smooth to slightly roughened, dry, grayish brown to dull brown, rupturing irregularly at maturity to expose the spore mass.

Spore mass: olive-brown to dark brown and powdery at maturity.

Microscopic features: spores 8–12 µm, globose, warted; brownish.

Fruiting: solitary, scattered, or in groups on the ground in fields, near gardens, along paths, and sometimes in woods; year-round; occasional to fairly common; widely distributed along the West Coast.

Dye notes:

no mordant	∘	light yellow-brown
alum	·	light yellow-brown
chrome	··	light brown
tin	···	pinkish brown
copper	····	golden brown
iron	·····	light brown

False Morels

False morels, also known as lorchels, include mushrooms with a brain-like, saddle-shaped, trilobate, mitre-shaped, shield-shaped, or irregularly lobed cap. The stalks of some species are small and terete to compressed or ribbed, while others are massive and multichambered.

Gyromitra esculenta (Persoon) Fries

Illus. p. 28

Cap: 1⅜–4" (3.5–10 cm) wide, 1½–4" (4–10 cm) tall, brain-like to irregularly lobed, deeply wrinkled to convoluted, moist to dry; margin undulating to contorted, often curved toward the stalk; fertile surface pinkish tan to dark reddish brown or orange-brown, lubricous when fresh; sterile surface pale pinkish tan to yellowish tan; interior chambered; flesh whitish, very brittle.

Stalk: ¾–2¾" (2–7 cm) long, ¾–1⅛" (2–3 cm) thick, enlarging downward or nearly equal, hollow or stuffed with cottony hyphae, sometimes chambered; surface smooth and waxy to slightly granular, dingy white to pinkish tan or tan, often ribbed near the base.

Microscopic features: spores 18–28 x 9–13 μm, elliptic, smooth, with 2 oil drops.

Fruiting: solitary, scattered or in groups on the ground under conifers; April–June; common; widely distributed in North America.

Dye notes:

no mordant	∘	none
alum	·	beige
chrome	··	pinkish beige
tin	···	orange
copper	····	light brown
iron	·····	beige

Gyromitra infula (Schaeffer) Quélet

Illus. p. 28

Cap: 1–4" (2.5–10 cm) wide, ¾–4" (2–10 cm) tall, usually saddle-shaped or sometimes trilobate, margin incurved; fertile surface wrinkled to convoluted or sometimes nearly smooth, moist when fresh, reddish brown to dark brown, lacking distinct violet to lavender tints; interior hollow or chambered; flesh brittle.

Stalk: ¾–2⅜" (2–6 cm) long, ¾–1" (2–2.5 cm) thick, dry, hollow, finely granular, whitish to pinkish buff.

Microscopic features: spores 18–23 x 7–10 μm, elliptic, smooth, hyaline, with two large oil drops when mounted in water; paraphyses commonly forked and strongly enlarged at their apices, reaching a diameter of 10 μm.

Fruiting: solitary, scattered or in groups on decaying wood or humus; July–October in the East, October–April in the West; occasional; widely distributed in North America.

Dye notes:

no mordant	∘	light beige
alum	·	light orange
chrome	··	brownish orange
tin	···	orange
copper	····	orange-brown
iron	·····	gray-brown

Fiber Fans and Vases

Fiber Fans and Vases, members of the genus *Thelephora,* are leathery, fibrous-tough fungi with split or torn margins and brown spores that are usually warted or spiny. Their fruiting bodies are typically some shade of brown at maturity. Some members have distinct caps with or without stalks, while others produce coral-like tufts of forking, spoon-shaped to flattened branches.

Thelephora palmata Scopoli : Fries

Illus. p. 29

Fruiting body: 1½–4" (4–10 cm) high, 1½–2¾" (4–7 cm) wide, coral-like, consisting of numerous branches arising from a short stalk; stalk short, up to ⅝" (1.5 cm) long and wide, colored like the branches, divided on the upper portion; branches smooth, flattened, palm-shaped, richly divided, whitish when very young, soon becoming grayish brown to lilac-brown or dark brown, often with purple to violet tints; branch tips usually whitish, conspicuously flattened and spatula-shaped, often finely fringed; flesh corky to fibrous-tough, brown; odor strongly foetid and disagreeable, especially after drying, rarely not distinctive.

Spore print: purplish brown.

Microscopic features: spores 8–12 x 6–9 μm, angular-lobate, strongly echinulate, brown.

Fruiting: solitary, scattered or in groups on the ground in conifer or mixed woods; July–October; occasional; widely distributed in North America.

Comments: *Thelephora anthocephala* is similar but its branches taper upward, the branch tips are not spatula-like and flattened, and its flesh lacks the foetid odor.

Dye notes:

no mordant	∘	light brown
alum	·	blackish brown
chrome	··	dark grayish green
tin	···	black
copper	····	greenish brown
iron	·····	brownish gray

Best results have been obtained using a 6:5 mushroom to wool ratio.

Thelephora terrestris Fries

Illus. p. 135

Fruiting body: partially erect and spreading, ¾–2" (2–5 cm) high, ½–2¾" (1.3–7 cm) wide, composed of circular to fan-shaped stalkless caps in overlapping clusters, often laterally fused and forming patches 12" (30.5 cm) or more in diameter; upper surface covered with short, stiff hairs, often matted and wooly or scaly, somewhat concentrically zoned, rusty brown to dark brown or grayish brown, becoming blackish brown in age; margin white or brown, wooly, coarsely torn, often with small fan-shaped outgrowths; lower surface somewhat wrinkled and finely warted, pinkish brown to brown.

Flesh: thin, leathery, watery brown; odor somewhat earthy or absent; taste not distinctive.

Spore print: purple-brown.

Microscopic features: spores 8–12 x 6–9 µm, angularly oval to elliptic, nearly smooth to warted or spiny, purplish.

Fruiting: solitary or in overlapping clusters attached to roots, branches, seedlings or mosses (especially sphagnum moss), or on the ground in conifer woods; year-round; common; eastern Canada south to Georgia, west across Canada and the northern United States.

Dye notes:

no mordant	∘	brown
alum	·	grayish brown
chrome	··	brown
tin	···	brownish gray
copper	····	brown
iron	·····	brown

Best results have been obtained using a 6:5 mushroom to wool ratio.

Thelephora terrestris f. *concrescens* Lundell

Illus. p. 135

Fruiting body: partially erect and enveloping the stems and branches of host plants, ½–2¾" (1.3–7 cm) wide, composed of circular to fan-shaped or funnel-shaped, stalkless caps in overlapping clusters, sometimes laterally fused and forming patches up to 10" (25 cm) or more in diameter; upper surface covered with short, stiff hairs, often matted and wooly or scaly, somewhat concentrically zoned, rusty brown to dark brown or grayish brown, becoming blackish brown in age; margin wavy or sometimes lobed, white to grayish when fresh; lower surface somewhat wrinkled and finely warted to nearly smooth; grayish to pinkish brown when young, becoming dull brown in age.

Flesh: thin, leathery, brown; odor somewhat earthy or absent; taste not distinctive.

Spore print: purplish brown.

Microscopic features: spores 8–12 x 6–9 µm, angularly oval to elliptic, warted and spiny, brown.

Fruiting: in overlapping clusters enveloping and clasping the stems and branches of woody plants, especially oak; July–December; occasional; Georgia and Florida west to Texas.

Dye notes:

no mordant	∘	light beige
alum	·	light grayish green
chrome	··	light grayish green
tin	···	light blue
copper	····	beige
iron	·····	light grayish green

Best results have been obtained using a 6:5 mushroom to wool ratio.

Thelephora vialis Schweinitz

Illus. p. 29

Fruiting body: erect, large, 1–4" (2.5–10 cm) tall, highly variable, typically composed of ascending lobes or caps clustered and arising from a common central stalk.

Cap: funnel- to spoon-shaped, or fused and somewhat vase-shaped, arising from a common central base; inner (upper) surface striate or minutely scaly, whitish to yellowish; outer (lower) surface wrinkled, dingy yellow then grayish brown.

Stalk: 3/8–2" (1–5 cm) long, 1/4–1 1/2" (5–40 mm) thick, erect, enlarged downward, dry, solid, whitish to grayish, minutely pubescent.

Flesh: thick, leathery, whitish to grayish; odor and taste not distinctive when fresh, odor becoming somewhat disagreeable on drying.

Spore print: brown.

Microscopic features: spores 4.5–8 x 4.5–6.5 µm, angular and warted, minutely spiny, olive-buff.

Fruiting: solitary, scattered or in groups on the ground in broadleaf woods, especially oak; August–November; occasional to fairly common; New England south to Florida, west to Texas and Illinois.

Dye notes:

no mordant	◦	light greenish beige
alum	·	greenish blue
chrome	··	grayish green
tin	···	bluish gray
copper	····	olive
iron	·····	dark bluish gray

Gilled Mushrooms

Gilled mushrooms, also known as agarics, belong to a very large group of fungi that have caps with knifeblade-like gills on the undersurface. Many have a central to eccentric stalk; others are laterally-stalked or stalkless. The cap diameter of some species rarely exceeds 1/8" (3 mm) at maturity, while others attain a diameter of 10" (25.5 cm) or more. A universal veil surrounds the button stage of some gilled mushrooms, often leaving warts and patches on the cap and a volva surrounding the stalk base. Many species produce a partial veil, often leaving a ring on the stalk at maturity.

Gilled mushrooms occur in a seemingly endless array of colors and sometimes change color as they mature. They grow on a wide varity of substrates, including soil, humus, wood, sawdust, straw, cones, fruits, manure, and other mushrooms.

European dyers often use only the caps of mushrooms, particularly when collecting various Cortinarius species, for the best color results. We have used the whole mushroom unless noted.

Anthracophyllum lateritium (Berkeley and Curtis) Singer Illus. p. 135

Cap: 1/4–1" (5–25 mm) wide, convex, shell- to kidney-shaped; surface dry, subtomentose to glabrous, radially rugose, pale reddish brown at first, becoming dark reddish brown in age; margin incurved at first, remaining so well into maturity, surpassing the gills; flesh pale yellowish brown; odor and taste not distinctive.

Gills: strongly arched, subdistant to distant, narrow, pale rusty brown to dark reddish brown, darkening in age, with two to three tiers of lamellulae.

Stalk: absent or rudimentary.

Spore print: white.

Microscopic features: spores 9.5–15 x 5.5–8 µm, oblong-ellipsoid to elongate-elipsoid with a tapered base, hyaline, inamyloid.

Fruiting: in groups or large masses on decaying hardwoods, especially oak; March–September; fairly common; along the Gulf Coast states from Florida to Texas.

Dye notes:

no mordant	◦	black
alum	·	black
chrome	··	black
tin	···	black
copper	····	black
iron	·····	black

Chroogomphus rutilus (Schaeffer : Fries) O. K. Miller, Jr.

Illus. p. 135

Cap: ¾–3⅛" (2–8 cm) wide, obtuse to convex, sometimes with a small pointed umbo; surface sticky when fresh, dull orange-brown to ochraceous-brown or pale reddish brown; margin incurved when young; flesh pale salmon to pale ochraceous or pinkish tinged; odor and taste not distinctive.

Gills: thick, decurrent, close to subdistant, broad, pale ochre when young, becoming pale cinnamon-brown in age.

Stalk: 2–6" (5–15.5 cm) long, ¼–1" (6–25 mm) thick, solid, tapered toward the base or nearly equal, ochraceous-buff to tawny-orange, often with vinaceous tints in age; partial veil pale ochraceous, fibrillose, sometimes leaving a thin layer of fibrils on the upper portion of the stalk.

Spore print: smoky gray to blackish.

Microscopic features: spores 14–22 x 6–7.5 µm, elliptic, smooth, pale gray-brown; cystidia thin-walled.

Fruiting: scattered or in groups on the ground under conifers; August–October; occasional; widely distributed in nothern and southwestern North America, and the West Coast.

Dye notes:

no mordant	◦	light brown
alum	·	light brown
chrome	··	pinkish brown
tin	···	brownish orange
copper	····	golden brown
iron	·····	brown

Chroogomphus vinicolor (Peck) O. K. Miller, Jr.

Illus. p. 135

Cap: ¾–3⅛" (2–8 cm) wide, convex to obtuse or sometimes with a small umbo; surface smooth, sticky when fresh, shiny when dry, color variable, vinaceous-red, orange-red or yellow-brown, often dark vinaceous red in age; flesh orange in young specimens, fading to ochraceous-buff or pale salmon in age; odor and taste not distinctive.

Gills: subdistant to distant, decurrent, buff to pale orange when young, becoming dull ochraceous then smoky brown in age.

Stalk: 2–5" (5–10 cm) long, ¼–¾" (6–20 mm) thick at the apex, tapered downward, dry, nearly smooth, pale ochraceous, becoming orange-buff to vinaceous-red in age; partial veil pale ochraceous, fibrillose, sometimes leaving a thin layer of fibrils on the upper portion of the stalk.

Spore print: smoky gray to dull olive-gray.

Microscopic features: spores 17–23 x 4.5–7.5 µm; cystidia with thickened walls, up to 7.5 µm thick in the midportion; cuticular hyphae 6–7 µm thick.

Fruiting: scattered or in groups on the ground or among mosses under conifers, especially pines; August–March; occasional to locally common; widely distributed across North America.

Comments: *Chroogomphus jamaicensis* (Murrill) O. K. Miller, Jr., is nearly identical but has slightly smaller spores, 17–20 x 4.5–6 µm, cystidia with more uniformly thickened walls, up to 5 µm thick, and cuticular hyphae which measure 2–5 µm wide.

Dye notes:

no mordant	∘	brownish pink
alum	·	brownish pink
chrome	··	pinkish brown
tin	···	golden brown
copper	····	greenish brown
iron	·····	pinkish brown

Collybia acervata (Fries) Kummer

Illus. p. 136

Cap: 1⅝–2" (1.5–5 cm) wide, convex when young, becoming broadly convex to nearly flat in age; surface smooth, dry to moist, hygrophanous, reddish brown to chestnut-brown when young, paler along the margin, fading in age to pale reddish brown with a light tan or buff margin; opaque, sometimes translucent-striate; flesh whitish; odor and taste not distinctive.

Gills: attached or notched, close to crowded, whitish with a pinkish tinge.

Stalk: 1½–4" (4–10 cm) long, ⅛–¼" (2–6 mm) thick, equal, hollow, brittle, dry, smooth, shiny, pale yellow-brown to purple-brown, reddish brown or brown, with white hairs toward the base.

Spore print: white to cream.

Microscopic features: spores 5.5–7 x 2.5–3 µm, lacrymoid to elliptic, smooth, hyaline, inamyloid.

Fruiting: in dense clusters or groups among sphagnum mosses in bogs, on decaying wood or on rich humus in conifer or mixed woods; July–October; occasional; northeastern North America, also recorded from Colorado and Texas.

Comments: also known as *Gymnopus acervatus.*

Dye notes:

no mordant	∘	none
alum	·	light beige
chrome	··	light grayish beige
tin	···	light yellow
copper	····	light golden brown
iron	·····	light grayish beige

Collybia iocephala (Berkeley and Curtis) Singer

Illus. p. 136

Cap: ½–1½" (1.2–4 cm) wide, convex, becoming broadly convex to plane in age, sometimes shallowly depressed; surface moist or dry, wrinkled and striate to sulcate nearly to the disc, color variable, violet, purple, vinaceous, fading to purplish lilac to pinkish lilac; margin inrolled at first, becoming uplifted and wavy in age; flesh purplish lilac to pinkish lilac; odor pungent and disagreeable; taste unpleasant.

Gills: adnate to adnexed, subdistant to distant, reddish purple to violet.

Stalk: ¾–2¾" (2–7 cm) long, 1⁄16–3⁄16" (1.5–4 mm) thick, enlarged downward or nearly equal, apex often expanded, dry, hollow, whitish or sometimes tinged pale pinkish lilac, minutely pubescent overall.

Spore print: white.

Microscopic features: spores 6.5–9 x 3–4.5 µm, ovoid, smooth, hyaline, inamyloid.

Macrochemical tests: cap, gills, and stalk stain bright blue with the application of KOH.

Fruiting: scattered or in groups on leaf litter and humus, August–October; infrequent to locally common; New England to Florida, west to Texas.

Comments: also known as *Gymnopus iocephalus.*

Dye notes:

no mordant	◦	light purple
alum	·	purple-blue
chrome	··	grayish purple
tin	···	gray
copper	····	greenish blue
iron	·····	grayish purple

Coprinus atramentarius (Bulliard : Fries) Fries

Illus. p. 136

Cap: 1½–3" (4–7.5 cm) wide, oval to egg-shaped when young, becoming convex in age; surface smooth to slightly scurfy, sometimes forming tiny scales on the disc, dry, gray to gray-brown, often with shallow grooves on the margin; flesh grayish white; odor and taste not distinctive.

Gills: free, very crowded, white when very young, soon gray then black and deliquescing to a black inky fluid in age.

Stalk: 1½–6" (4–15.5 cm) long, ⅜–¾" (1–2 cm) thick, nearly equal or tapered downward, silky, hollow in age, white, with a white annular zone toward the base.

Spore print: black.

Microscopic features: spores 8–12 x 4.5–6 µm, elliptic, smooth, with an apical pore, pale grayish black.

Fruiting: in clusters on grass, wood chips and tree bases, May–November; very common; widely distributed in North America.

Dye notes:

no mordant	◦	beige
alum	·	beige
chrome	··	beige
tin	···	beige
copper	····	beige
iron	·····	beige

Coprinus micaceus (Bulliard : Fries) Fries

Illus. p. 136

Cap: ¾–2" (2–5 cm) wide, oval to egg-shaped when young, becoming bell-shaped to convex in age; surface covered with a sparse coating of tiny whitish granular scales on the button stage and soon becoming smooth, weakly to distinctly sulcate from the margin nearly to the disc, tawny to orange-brown on the disc, yellowish tan toward the margin, becoming grayish to dark grayish brown in age; flesh whitish; odor and taste not distinctive.

Gills: attached to nearly free, very crowded, white when young, soon gray then black and deliquescing to a black inky fluid in age.

Stalk: 1–3⅛" (2.5–8 cm) long, ⅛–¼" (2–5 mm) thick, equal, smooth, hollow in age, white, lacking an annular zone.

Spore print: black.

Microscopic features: spores 7–10 x 4–5 µm, elliptic with an apical pore, smooth, pale grayish black.

Fruiting: in dense clusters on lawns or decaying wood; April–October; very common; widely distributed in North America.

Dye notes:

no mordant	∘	beige
alum	·	pinkish beige
chrome	··	pinkish beige
tin	···	light brown
copper	····	greenish beige
iron	·····	beige

Cortinarius armillatus (Fries) Kummer

Illus. p. 136

Cap: 2–4¾" (5–12 cm) wide, bell-shaped when young, becoming broadly convex to nearly flat with a low broad umbo in age; surface moist to dry, covered with tiny fibrils, nearly smooth, reddish brown to brownish orange; margin incurved when young, expanded in age, sometimes with veil remnants attached; flesh yellowish buff to pale tawny; odor not distinctive or like radishes, taste not distinctive or slightly bitter.

Gills: attached, distant, broad, tawny, becoming rusty brown in age.

Stalk: 2¾–5⅞" (7–15 cm) long, ⅜–1" (1–2.5 cm) thick, enlarged downward to a bulbous or club-shaped base, solid, fibrous, whitish to pale brown, with multiple cinnabar-red rings or zones; partial veil cortinate, whitish, leaving a thin, fibrous annular zone on the upper portion of the stalk.

Spore print: rusty brown.

Microscopic features: spores 7–12 x 5–7 µm, elliptic to almond-shaped, with warts, pale brown.

Fruiting: solitary or in groups on the ground or among mosses under conifers and hardwoods, especially birch and pine; August–October; fairly common; eastern Canada south to New England, west to British Columbia, south to California.

Dye notes:

no mordant	∘	pinkish beige
alum	·	pinkish beige
chrome	··	light beige
tin	···	beige
copper	····	light greenish beige
iron	·····	dark beige

Cortinarius badius Peck

Illus. p. 136

Cap: ⅜–1⅛" (1–3 cm) wide, conical to bell-shaped when young, becoming broadly convex in age, conspicuously umbonate, surface appressed-fibrillose to fibrillose-scaly, moist and hygrophanous when fresh, dark chestnut-brown to mahagony-brown, becoming paler reddish brown to chestnut in age, sometimes with a gray tinge, darker on the umbo; margin incurved at first, becoming decurved, often lacerated and deeply sulcate toward the disc in age or when drying; flesh colored like the cap, odor and taste not distinctive.

Gills: adnexed, subdistant, broad, yellowish or cream-color at first, becoming subochraceous then rusty brown at maturity.

Stalk: ¾–2" (2–5 cm) long, ¹⁄₁₆–⅛" (1.5–4 cm) wide, nearly equal down to a slightly enlarged base, dry, solid at first but soon hollow, silky-fibrillose, colored like the cap; basal mycelium white; partial veil cortinate, whitish, leaving a superior evanescent ring.

Spore print: rusty brown.

Microscopic features: spores 10.5–13 x 6.5–7.5 μm, broadly elliptic, finely warted, pale brown.

Fruiting: scattered or in groups on the ground among mosses under conifers, especially pines; August–October; occasional; throughout Northeastern North America.

Dye notes:

no mordant	∘	light beige
alum	·	beige
chrome	··	grayish beige
tin	···	light golden brown
copper	····	golden brown
iron	·····	light golden brown

Cortinarius bolaris Fries

Illus. p. 137

Cap: 1⅛–2⅜" (3–6 cm) wide, convex when young, becoming broadly convex in age; surface dry, whitish, covered overall with reddish to orange-red hairs and scales; margin incurved when young, remaining so well into maturity, surpassing the gills; flesh white with tints of pale yellow; odor and taste not distinctive.

Gills: attached, close, moderately broad, pale buff, becoming pale cinnamon-brown.

Stalk: 1½–2⅜" (4–6 cm) long, ¼–⅜" (5–10 mm) thick, enlarged downward to a bulbous base, hollow in age, whitish, covered by reddish to orange-red fibers and flattened scales, staining yellow to reddish when bruised; partial veil cortinate, white, leaving a thin, fibrous annular zone on the upper portion of the stalk.

Spore print: rusty brown.

Microscopic features: spores 6–7 x 5–5.5 μm, oval to subglobose, slightly roughened, pale brown.

Fruiting: in groups or clusters on the ground under conifers and in mixed woods; August–October; infrequent; widely distributed in eastern North America.

Dye notes:

no mordant	∘	pinkish brown
alum	·	yellow-brown
chrome	··	light yellow-green
tin	···	olive
copper	····	greenish brown
iron	·····	brown

Cortinarius brunneus (Persoon) Fries

Illus. p. 137

Cap: 1⅛–4½ (3–11.5 cm) wide, bell-shaped to conical when young, becoming broadly convex to nearly plane in age, usually with a conspicuous umbo; surface moist, glabrous, hygrophanous and remaining darkest over the disc, dark chestnut-brown to reddish brown or grayish brown; margin incurved at first, becoming decurved and wrinkled to somewhat sulcate at maturity; flesh brownish; odor faintly to distinctly radish-like; taste not distinctive.

Gills: attached, subdistant, wide, purplish brown to dark brown at first, becoming reddish brown at maturity.

Stalk: 2–5½" (5–14 cm) long, ¼–¾" (7–20 mm) thick, nearly equal or slightly enlarged toward the base, solid, becoming hollow in age, dry, fibrillose, whitish at first, darkening to brown from the base upward in age or when bruised; partial veil cortinate, whitish, leaving a superior ring.

Spore print: rusty brown.

Microscopic features: spores 7.5–9 x 5–6.5 µm, broadly ellipsoid, finely warted, brown.

Fruiting: scattered or in groups on the ground and among mosses under conifers, especially spruce; August–November; fairly common; northeastern North America.

Dye notes:

no mordant	∘	none
alum	·	beige
chrome	··	beige
tin	···	light brown
copper	····	light brown
iron	·····	beige

Cortinarius californicus A. H. Smith

Illus. p. 137

Cap: 1–3" (2.5–7.5 cm) wide, convex, becoming broadly convex with a broad umbo in age; surface dry, smooth or nearly so, hygrophanous, dark rusty red to dull orange-red or brownish red, margin even; flesh thin, orange-red; odor and taste not distinctive.

Gills: adnate to adnexed, subdistant, pale reddish orange at first, darkening to rusty orange and finally rusty red at maturity.

Stalk: 2–6" (5–15 cm) long, ⅛–⅜" (4–11 mm) thick, nearly equal, dry, solid, fibrillose, pale yellowish orange to dull orange or orange-red, with an orange-red basal mycelium; partial veil dull orange, evanescent or leaving a faint annular zone.

Spore print: rusty brown.

Microscopic features: spores 7–10 x 5–6 µm, ellipsoid to ovoid, warty and wrinkled, dark rusty brown.

Fruiting: scattered or in groups on the ground under conifers, especially spruce and fir; September–January; occasional; California and Oregon.

Comments: *Cortinarius phoeniceus* var. *occidentalis* (Bulliard) A. H. Smith is very similar but its cap is fibrillose to silky and its cap, gills, and stalk are darker red. Several other red *Cortinarius* species may also be confused with this species.

Dye notes:

no mordant	∘	pinkish orange to light purple
alum	·	dark orange-pink
chrome	··	brownish purple

tin	···	brownish pink
copper	····	reddish purple
iron	·····	purplish pink

A good dyer, it would be worth experimenting using a 3:5 ratio of mushroom to yarn, or even a 2:5 ratio.

Cortinarius cinnamomeus Fries

Illus. p. 137

Cap: ¾–1¾" (2–4.5 cm) wide, campanulate-convex to broadly convex, often with an umbo; surface dry, appressed-fibrillose to silky, usually shiny, yellowish tawny to yellowish cinnamon, margin even; flesh thin, pale greenish yellow to straw-yellow or darker; odor and taste not distinctive.

Gills: adnate to adnexed or sometimes subdecurrent, close, orange at first, becoming cinnamon-orange to rusty brown at maturity.

Stalk: 1⅛–3⅛" (3–8 cm) long, ⅛–¼" (3–6 mm) thick, nearly equal, dry, hollow at maturity, fibrillose, yellow to greenish yellow when fresh, becoming brownish in age or when handled, with a yellow basal mycelium; partial veil fibrillose, greenish yellow, evanescent and typically leaving a faint annular zone.

Spore print: rusty brown.

Microscopic features: spores 6–9 x 4–5 μm, elliptical, minutely roughened, brownish.

Fruiting: scattered or in groups on the ground under conifers, especially pine; September–March; fairly common; widely distributed across North America.

Dye notes:

no mordant	◦	light brown
alum	·	pinkish brown
chrome	··	pinkish brown
tin	···	golden brown
copper	····	brownish green
iron	·····	light brown

Cortinarius corrugatus Peck

Illus. p. 137

Cap: 1⅜–4" (3–10 cm) wide, bluntly conic to bell-shaped, becoming broadly convex in age; surface smooth, shiny, viscid, with distinct radial corrugations, rusty ochraceous to ochre-tawny; flesh white; odor and taste not distinctive.

Gills: attached, close, broad, purplish at first, becoming rusty cinnamon at maturity; edges often eroded in age.

Stalk: 2–4⅜" (5–11 cm) long, ¼–⅝" (6–16 mm) thick, nearly equal down to an enlarged and sometimes bulbous base, typically scurfy overall, moist or dry, tawny to ochraceous; partial veil cortinate, leaving a sparse annular zone or evanescent.

Spore print: rusty brown.

Microscopic features: spores 10–14 x 7–9 μm, elliptic, roughened, pale brown.

Fruiting: solitary, scattered or in groups on the ground under hardwoods, especially oak and beech, or in mixed woods; July–October; occasional; throughout eastern North America.

Dye notes:

no mordant	∘	none
alum	·	beige
chrome	··	beige
tin	···	light yellow
copper	····	greenish beige
iron	·····	beige

Cortinarius croceofolius Peck

Illus. p. 137

Cap: 1–2" (2.5–5 cm) wide, bell-shaped when young, becoming broadly convex to nearly flat with a low broad umbo in age; surface dry, covered with minute hairs and scales, dark orange to saffron-yellow when young, becoming dark brownish to cinnamon-orange in age, remaining darkest over the disc, fading to orange toward the margin; margin incurved when young, remaining so into maturity; flesh yellowish; odor and taste not distinctive.

Gills: attached, close, narrow, orange when young, becoming brownish orange to cinnamon in age.

Stalk: 1–2" (2.5–5 cm) long, ¼–½" (6–12 mm) thick, enlarged downward, hollow, yellow to yellowish brown, often reddish at the base; partial veil cortinate, yellow, leaving a thin, fibrous annular zone on the upper portion of the stalk.

Spore print: rusty brown.

Microscopic features: spores 6–7.5 x 4–5 μm, elliptic, roughened, pale brown.

Fruiting: solitary, scattered or in groups on the ground under conifers; September–November; occasional to locally common; New England and New York west to the Pacific Northwest.

Comments: also known as *Cortinarius malicorius* Fries.

Dye notes:

no mordant	∘	light orange
alum	·	light orange
chrome	··	unknown
tin	···	brownish orange
copper	····	dark brownish orange
iron	·····	dark brownish orange

A good dyer, worth experimenting with a 3:5 or 2:5 ratio of mushroom to wool.

Cortinarius croceus (Schaeffer) Gray

Illus. p. 138

Cap: ¾–3" (2–7.5 cm) wide, hemispherical to bell-shaped when young, becoming broadly convex to nearly flat, usually with a low broad umbo in age; surface dry, covered with minute hairs or scales, especially towards the margin, yellowish brown to reddish brown, paler near the margin or sometimes overall; margin decurved when young and often remaining so into maturity; flesh pale to dark yellow, darker toward the base of the stalk, sometimes with a greenish tint; odor faint, radish-like or resembling iodine; taste not distinctive.

Gills: attached, close to somewhat crowded, narrow, yellow at first, becoming ochraceous-yellow to yellow-orange, darkening in age.

Stalk: 1⅛–4" (3–10 cm) long, ⅛–⅜" (3–10 mm) thick, nearly equal overall, hollow at maturity, golden yellow to ochraceous-yellow, becoming brownish yellow in age; partial veil cortinate, yellow, leaving a thin, fibrous annular zone on the upper portion of the stalk that becomes reddish brown as the spores mature.

Spore print: rusty brown.

Microscopic features: spores 6.5–9 x 4–5.5 µm, broadly ellipsoid, distinctly roughened, pale brown.

Fruiting: solitary, scattered or in groups on the ground, usually under conifers; August–November; fairly common; widely distributed in North America.

Comments: Often misidentified as *Cortinarius cinnamomeus,* which has orange gills from the beginning.

Dye notes:

no mordant	∘	light brown
alum	·	light pinkish brown
chrome	··	pinkish brown
tin	···	light brownish gold
copper	····	light golden brown
iron	·····	light brown

Cortinarius limonius Fries

Illus. p. 138

Cap: ¾–3⅛" (2–8 cm) wide, convex when young, becoming broadly convex to nearly plane in age, often broadly unbonate; surface dry, glabrous overall or slightly scaly near the margin, sometimes wrinkled, hygrophanous, bright reddish brown to reddish orange when moist, becoming bright brownish yellow when dry; margin incurved at first, becoming decurved at maturity; flesh yellow, becoming yellow-brown in the stalk from the base upward; odor and taste not distinctive.

Gills: sinuate, close to somewhat crowded, broad, yellow at first, becoming brownish yellow to ochraceous-brown.

Stalk: 1–3½" (2.5–9 cm) long, ⅜–¾" (1–2 cm) thick, nearly equal or enlarged downward to a tapered and frequently curved base, dry, hollow in age, fibrillose, yellow on the upper portion, becoming yellowish- to reddish brown from the base upward in age or when bruised; partial veil cortinate, yellow, leaving indistinct rings on the upper stalk.

Spore print: rusty brown.

Microscopic features: spores 7–9 x 6–7 µm, broadly ellipsoid to subglobose, slightly roughened, pale brown.

Fruiting: scattered or in groups on the ground under conifers and in mixed woods; July–October; occasional to fairly common; northeastern North America.

Comments: *Cortinarius limonius* and *Cortinarius whitei* Peck are synonyms according to Phillips (1991).

Dye notes:

no mordant	∘	light yellow
alum	·	yellow
chrome	··	light brownish yellow
tin	···	light orange
copper	····	brownish yellow
iron	·····	light grayish brown

Cortinarius marylandensis Ammirati and Smith

Illus. p. 138

Cap: 1–2⅜" (2.5–6 cm) wide, bell-shaped when young, becoming broadly convex to flat with a low, broad umbo in age; surface dry, smooth, shiny or dull, somewhat felty, bright reddish orange to reddish brown; margin somewhat incurved when young, becoming expanded and often split in age; flesh yellowish; odor and taste not distinctive.

Gills: attached, subdistant, broad, cinnabar-red when young, fading to cinnamon-brown in age.

Stalk: ¾–2¾" (2–7 cm) long, ⅛–⅜" (3–10 mm) thick, equal or enlarged slightly downward toward the base, dry, hollow, streaked with reddish orange to reddish brown fibrils over a reddish yellow ground color, often yellowish to whitish at the base; partial veil cortinate, reddish, leaving a thin, fibrous annular zone on the upper portion of the stalk.

Spore print: rusty brown.

Microscopic features: spores 7–9 x 4–5 μm, elliptic, slightly roughened, pale brown.

Macrochemical tests: cap stains rose then purple with the application of KOH.

Fruiting: scattered or in groups on the ground under conifers and hardwoods, especially oak and beech; August–October; occasional; widely distributed in North America.

Comments: *Cortinarius cinnabarinus* is nearly identical but its cap does not stain rose then purple when KOH is applied.

Dye notes:

no mordant	∘	light purple
alum	·	dark red
chrome	··	purple
tin	···	red
copper	····	brownish purple
iron	·····	bluish purple

A very fine dye mushroom. Try a 3:5 or 2:5 ratio of mushroom to wool.

Cortinarius phoeniceus var. *occidentalis* A. H. Smith

Illus. p. 138

Cap: 1⅛–3⅛" (3–8 cm) wide, broadly convex, becoming nearly plane with an umbo in age, margin decurved; surface dry, silky to appressed-fibrillose, dark red to brownish red or maroon-red; flesh reddish near the cap surface, pale olive-brown near the stalk; odor and taste not distinctive or slightly radish-like.

Gills: red to dark red or vinaceous-red at first, becoming rusty red to reddish brown at maturity, adnate to adnexed, close to subdistant.

Stalk: 1½–3½" (4–9 cm) long, ¼–½" (6–12 mm) thick, nearly equal, dry, solid, fibrillose, ochre to dull golden yellow; partial veil pale yellow to yellow, evanescent or leaving a sparse superior annular zone; basal mycelium yellow-ochre, sometimes tinged vinaceous-red.

Spore print: rusty brown.

Microscopic features: spores 6–8 x 4–5, elliptic and pointed at one end, minutely roughened, brownish.

Fruiting: solitary, scattered, or in groups on the ground under conifers or hardwoods; October–February; fairly common; West Coast.

Dye notes: *

no mordant	◦	pinkish orange
alum	·	purplish red
chrome	··	dark purplish red
tin	···	red
copper	····	grayish purple
iron	·····	dark bluish purple to bluish black

We suspect that a 3:5 ratio of mushroom to wool would produce fine color results.

Cortinarius sanguineus Fries

Illus. p. 138

Cap: 1–2⅜" (2.5–6 cm) wide, bell-shaped when young, becoming broadly convex to plane, often with a low, broad umbo in age; surface dry, smooth, shiny or dull, fibrillose to silky, dark red to blood-red, margin somewhat incurved when young, becoming expanded and sometimes split in age; flesh blood-red to reddish purple; odor not distinctive; taste slightly like radish or not distinctive.

Gills: adnate to adnexed, close, cinnabar-red to blood-red when young, becoming cinnamon-red to cinnamon-brown in age.

Stalk: 1⅛–4" (3–10 cm) long, ⅛–5⁄16" (3–8 mm) thick, equal or slightly enlarged downward, dry, hollow at maturity, colored like the cap or darker, usually with a yellowish to yellow-orange basal mycelium; partial veil cortinate, reddish, leaving a thin, fibrous annular zone on the upper portion of the stalk.

Spore print: rusty brown.

Microscopic features: spores 6–9 x 4–6 μm, elliptic, slightly roughened, pale brown.

Fruiting: scattered or in groups on the ground under conifers; August–November; occasional; widely distributed across North America.

Dye notes:

no mordant	◦	brownish orange
alum	·	purplish red
chrome	··	reddish purple
tin	···	red
copper	····	reddish brown
iron	·····	dark brown

An excellent dye mushroom. A 3:5 ratio of mushroom to wool produces fine color results.

Cortinarius scaurus Fries

Illus. p. 138

Cap: 1⅛–3⅛" (3–8 cm) wide, convex to obtuse or subumbonate at first, becoming nearly plane to slightly depressed in age; surface viscid, glabrous, yellowish brown when young, becoming tawny and sometimes with dark brown spots, especially on the disc at maturity; margin incurved and slightly fibrillose at first, becoming decurved and even or short-striate at maturity; flesh brownish; odor and taste not distinctive.

Gills: adnexed then emarginate, crowded to subdistant, narrow, greenish at first, becoming tawny-olive at maturity; edges even.

Stalk: 2⅜–4" (6–10 cm) long, ¼–⅜" (7–11 mm) thick, slightly enlarged or nearly equal down to a marginate, subdepressed bulbous base, dry, solid, fibrillose-silky, bluish green at the apex when fresh, whitish to ochraceous below, bulb whitish to pale straw-yellow; partial veil yellowish, leaving a sparse superior annular zone.

Spore print: rusty brown.
Microscopic features: spores 8–10 x 5–6 µm, ellipsoid, slightly roughened, rusty brown.
Fruiting: solitary, scattered or in groups on the ground under conifers or in mixed woods; August–October; occasional; widely distributed in the northern United States and Canada.
Comments: *Cortinarius herpeticus* is very similar but has a white to whitish bulbous base, a thicker stalk apex (1–2 cm), and broader gills.
Dye notes:

no mordant	◦	light yellow
alum	·	beige
chrome	··	yellow-beige
tin	···	yellow
copper	····	greenish beige
iron	·····	beige

Cortinarius semisanguineus (Fries) Gillet

Illus. p. 139

Cap: ¾–2⅜" (2–6 cm) wide, bell-shaped to convex when young, becoming broadly convex to nearly flat, with a low broad umbo in age; surface dry, covered with tiny matted fibrils, yellow-brown to cinnamon-buff, darker over the disc in age; margin incurved when young, becoming expanded; flesh whitish to yellowish; odor not distinctive; taste not distinctive or slightly bitter.
Gills: attached, crowded, narrow, dark blood-red to cinnabar.
Stalk: ¾–3" (2–7.5 cm) long, ⅛–¼" (3–6 mm) thick, equal, solid, fibrous, dull yellow, often reddish at the base and whitish at the apex, fibrillose; partial veil cortinate, yellowish, leaving a thin, fibrous annular zone on the upper portion of the stalk.
Spore print: rusty brown.
Microscopic features: spores 5–8 x 3–5 µm, elliptic, roughened, pale brown.
Fruiting: scattered or in groups on the ground or among mosses under hardwoods and conifers; July–November; fairly common; widely distributed in North America.
Dye notes:

no mordant	◦	pinkish beige
alum	·	purple-red
chrome	··	pinkish purple
tin	···	red
copper	····	purple
iron	·····	grayish purple

One of the most sought after dye mushrooms because of the rich colors it produces. A 3:5 ratio of mushroom to wool produces fine color results.

Cortinarius tubarius var. *luteofolius* Ammirati and A. H. Smith

Illus. p. 139

Cap: ¾–2" (2–5 cm) wide, obtusely conic to campanulate, becoming broadly conic to nearly plane, umbonate; surface moist, appressed-fibrillose to fibrillose-scaly, olivaceous at first, becoming brownish olive then reddish brown; margin incurved at first, becoming decurved, entire; flesh pale dull yellow to watery dull yellow; odor and taste radish-like.
Gills: adnexed or attached to subdecurrent, seceding in age, close, wide, yellow at first, becoming yellowish olive and finally brown with a yellowish tint at maturity.

Stalk: 2⅜–6" (6–15.5 cm) long, ⅛–½" (3–12 mm) thick, nearly equal or slightly enlarged toward the base, solid, becoming hollow in age, moist, appressed-fibrillose, yellow-olive becoming brown to rusty brown in age, with a yellow apex and whitish to yellowish tomentose base; partial veil cortinate, yellowish, leaving a superior evanescent ring.

Spore print: rusty brown.

Microscopic features: spores 9–12 x 4.5–6.5 μm, elliptic to ovate, rugose to verruculose, pale brown.

Fruiting: scattered or in groups among sphagnum mosses under conifers and in bogs; August–November; common; eastern Canada south to New York, west to Minnesota.

Comments: *Cortinarius tubarius* var. *tubarius* is very similar but its gills are light yellowish green to dull yellowish olive when immature, not yellow.

Dye notes:

no mordant	◦	light golden brown
alum	·	light pinkish brown
chrome	··	brownish pink
tin	···	pinkish orange
copper	····	golden brown
iron	·····	light brown

Cortinarius tubarius var. *tubarius* Ammirati and A. H. Smith Illus. p. 139

Cap: ¾–2" (2–5 cm) wide, obtusely conic to campanulate, becoming broadly conic to nearly plane, umbonate; surface moist or dry, appressed-fibrillose to fibrillose-scaly, dull yellowish olive at first, becoming dull olive-brown; margin incurved at first, becoming decurved, sometimes torn in age; flesh dull yellowish olive to watery dull olive; odor and taste radish-like or not distinctive.

Gills: adnexed, seceding in age, close to subdistant, wide, light yellowish green to dull yellowish olive at first, becoming dark yellow-brown to dull fulvous at maturity.

Stalk: 2⅜–6" (6–15.5 cm) long, ⅛–½" (3–12 mm) thick, nearly equal or slightly enlarged toward the base, solid, becoming hollow in age, moist, appressed-fibrillose, dull yellow, becoming dull yellowish olive to dull olive-brown, with a whitish tomentose base; partial veil cortinate, yellowish, leaving a superior evanescent ring.

Spore print: rusty brown.

Microscopic features: spores 9–12 x 5–6.5 μm, elliptic to ovate, rugose to verruculose, pale brown.

Fruiting: scattered or in groups among sphagnum mosses under conifers and in bogs; August–November; common; eastern Canada south to New York, west to Minnesota.

Comments: *Cortinarius tubarius* var. *luteofolius* is very similar but its gills are yellow when immature.

Dye notes:

no mordant	◦	beige
alum	·	pinkish beige
chrome	··	pinkish beige
tin	···	orange
copper	····	light brown
iron	·····	light greenish brown

Cortinarius violaceus (Fries) Gray

Illus. p. 139

Cap: 2–4¾" (5–12 cm) wide, convex when young, becoming broadly convex to nearly flat in age, with or without a small umbo; surface dry, covered with fibers that form minute erect tufts or scales, especially over the disc, dark violet to purple; margin incurved when young, expanded in age; flesh dark violet to grayish; odor and taste not distinctive.

Gills: attached, subdistant, broad, dark violet, becoming grayish cinnamon-brown.

Stalk: 2¾–5½" (7–14 cm) long, ⅜–1" (1–2.5 cm) thick, enlarged downward to a club-shaped base, solid, dry, covered with tiny matted fibrils, dark violet to purplish; partial veil cortinate, violet, leaving a thin, fibrous annular zone.

Spore print: rusty brown to rusty cinnamon.

Microscopic features: spores 12–17 x 8–10 μm, elliptic, roughened or with warts, pale brown.

Fruiting: solitary, scattered or in groups on the ground or among mosses under conifers; September–October; fairly common; widely distributed in North America.

Dye notes: *

no mordant	◦	light gray
alum	·	gray
chrome	··	light brown
tin	···	light brown
copper	····	grayish brown
iron	·····	gray

Flammulina velutipes (Fries) Karsten

Illus. p. 139

Cap: ¾–2¾" (2–7 cm) wide, convex becoming nearly flat; orangish brown to reddish yellow, darker at the center; smooth, slimy, very sticky when dry; margin incurved at first, becoming striate; flesh thin, yellowish, usually watery; odor and taste not distinctive.

Gills: attached becoming subdecurrent, yellowish, typically close and narrow.

Stalk: usually 1–3" (2.5–7.5 cm) long but sometimes longer, ⅛–¼" (3–7 mm) thick; smooth and yellowish at the top, becoming dark reddish brown and extremely velvety starting at the base; very tough, not easily broken.

Spore print: white.

Microscopic features: spores 7–9 x 3–6 μm, elliptic, smooth, hyaline, inamyloid.

Fruiting: in clusters on deciduous trees, logs and stumps, especially willow, aspen, poplar and elm; usually fruiting during early spring or late fall but also during winter thaws and summer cold spells; fairly common; widely distributed in North America.

Dye notes:

no mordant	◦	none
alum	·	beige
chrome	··	beige
tin	···	light orange
copper	····	greenish beige
iron	·····	beige

Gomphidius glutinosus (Schaeffer : Fries) Fries Illus. p. 139

Cap: ¾–4" (2–10 cm) wide, convex becoming broadly convex to nearly flat; surface smooth, slimy; color variable, grayish brown to purplish gray, pale cinnamon-gray, vinaceous-brown or pale salmon, typically spotted black in age; flesh thick, whitish, often tinted pink; odor not distinctive; taste acidic.

Gills: decurrent, thick, close, broad, pale grayish white, becoming smoky gray at maturity.

Stalk: 1⅜–4" (3.5–10 cm) long, ¼–¾" (7–20 mm) thick, tapered downward, solid, white with a yellow base; partial veil slimy, with white fibrils beneath the glutinous layer, leaving a thin slimy superior ring on the stalk, blackening as spores are trapped.

Spore print: smoky gray to blackish.

Microscopic features: spores 15–21 x 4–7 µm, elliptic, smooth, grayish brown.

Fruiting: solitary, scattered or in groups on the ground in conifer woods; June–November; occasional; widely distributed across the northern United States and Canada, and the West Coast.

Dye notes: *

no mordant	∘	light brown
alum	·	brown
chrome	··	brown
tin	···	brown
copper	····	dark brown
iron	·····	grayish brown

Gomphidius subroseus Kauffman Illus. p. 140

Cap: 1½–3" (4–7.5 cm) wide, obtuse to convex, becoming broadly convex in age, margin incurved and remaining so well into maturity; surface conspicuously glutinous, glabrous, rosy pink to dull red or yellowish red, typically paler pink toward the margin; flesh white with a pinkish tinge near the surface, dull white below; odor and taste not distinctive.

Gills: decurrent, close to subdistant, whitish at first, becoming smoky gray at maturity.

Stalk: 1⅛–2¾" (3–7 cm) long, ¼–¾" (6–20 mm) thick, tapered downward or nearly equal down to a tapered base, solid, silky near the apex, white down to a yellow or orange-yellow base; partial veil glutinous, colorless, leaving a superior glutinous ring that typically blackens as it traps spores.

Spore print: brownish black to black.

Microscopic features: spores 14–20 x 4.5–7 µm, elliptic, smooth, grayish brown.

Fruiting: solitary, scattered, or in groups on the ground under conifers; June–February; fairly common; western North America.

Dye notes: *

no mordant	∘	beige
alum	·	beige
chrome	··	beige
tin	···	brown
copper	····	light brown
iron	·····	beige

Gymnopilus liquiritiae (Persoon) Karsten

Illus. p. 140

Cap: ¾–3⅛" (2–8 cm) wide, convex, becoming broadly convex to nearly plane in age, sometimes slightly umbonate; surface moist or dry, not viscid, glabrous or nearly so, fulvous to ochraceous-tawny or ochraceous-orange to orange-brown; flesh pale orange to tawny-yellow; odor not distinctive or sometimes slightly fragrant or resembling raw potatoes; taste bitter.

Gills: adnate to adnexed, seceding, close to crowded, at first ochraceous-buff to pale orange-yellow, becoming ochraceous-orange to ochraceous-tawny or orange, sometimes with reddish brown spots, edges fimbriate.

Stalk: 1⅛–2¾" (3–7 cm) long, ⅛–⅜" (3–10 mm) thick, tapered in either direction or nearly equal, dry, hollow, longitudinally fibrillose or subglabrous, whitish to dingy orange, with a whitish or yellowish apex; partial veil and ring absent.

Spore print: rusty brown.

Microscopic features: spores 7–10 x 4–6 μm, ellipsoid, verruculose, lacking a germ pore, ferruginous, dextrinoid.

Fruiting: scattered or in groups on decaying conifer wood or sawdust, occasionally on decaying wood of broadleaf trees; June–January; occasional; widely distributed across North America.

Dye notes:

no mordant	◦	yellow
alum	·	gold
chrome	··	brownish orange
tin	···	orange
copper	····	golden brown
iron	·····	greenish yellow

Gymnopilus luteofolius (Peck) Singer

Illus. p. 140

Cap: ¾–3⅛" (2–8 cm) wide, obtuse to convex, becoming broadly convex in age, margin fibrillose to fibrillose-scaly, incurved and remaining so well into maturity, even; surface dry, covered with conspicuous erect to slightly recurved scales; scales dark reddish purple to purplish red on a tawny ground color when young, fading to rusty cinnamon to fulvous or dingy yellow at maturity; flesh pale purplish vinaceous to pale pinkish salmon on young specimens, yellow at maturity; odor not distinctive; taste bitter.

Gills: attached to decurrent, close, dull yellow at first, becoming dingy orange-yellow then rusty orange at maturity.

Stalk: 1⅛–3¾" (3–9.5 cm) long, ⅛–½" (3–12 mm) thick, nearly equal or enlarged downward, dry, hollow in age, longitudinally striate, fibrillose, apex pale to dull yellow, instantly staining pinkish red when bruised, dark reddish purple below when young, becoming dull reddish brown in age; partial veil fibrillose, yellowish, leaving a thin superior fibrillose annular zone; mycelium whitish to pale yelow.

Spore print: bright rusty orange.

Microscopic features: spores 5.5–8.5 x 3.5–4.5 μm, ellipsoid to subovoid, smooth, ochraceous, dextrinoid.

Fruiting: in dense clusters on decaying wood chips, logs, stumps and sawdust; June–January; occasional; widely distributed across North America.

Dye notes:

no mordant	◦	light yellow
alum	·	gold
chrome	··	brownish orange
tin	···	light brownish orange
copper	····	golden brown
iron	·····	light olive

Gymnopilus luteus (Peck) Hesler

Illus. p. 140

Cap: 2–4" (5–10 cm) wide, convex, becoming broadly convex in age; surface dry, appressed floccose-fibrillose to silky, buff-yellow to pale orange-yellow or ochre-orange, often with brownish tints over the disc; margin incurved at first and long remaining so, with a narrow band of sterile tissue; flesh pale yellow; odor of anise or licorice, sometimes slight; taste bitter.

Gills: adnexed, close, pale yellow at first, becoming rusty brown at maturity.

Stalk: 1½–3" (4–7.5 cm) long, ¼–⅝" (6–16 mm) thick, enlarged downward to a pinched base, typically expanded at the apex, dry, solid, fibrillose, colored like the cap, becoming rusty yellow when handled; partial veil fibrous to submembranous, pale yellow, leaving a superior, fibrillose annular zone.

Spore print: dull orange to rusty orange.

Microscopic features: spores 6–10 x 4–5.5 μm, ellipsoid to oval, finely warted, with a germ pore, ferruginious, dextrinoid.

Fruiting: clustered or scattered on decaying wood or on the ground arising from buried wood; August–October; occasional; eastern Canada south to the Carolinas, west to Tennessee, distribution limits yet to be established.

Comments: *Gymnopilus spectabilis* (Fries) A. H. Smith is nearly identical but its gills are adnate to decurrent.

Dye notes:

no mordant	◦	yellow
alum	·	light brownish orange
chrome	··	orange-brown
tin	···	brownish orange
copper	····	golden brown
iron	·····	olive

Gymnopilus penetrans (Fries) Murrill

Illus. p. 140

Cap: ¾–2" (2–5 cm) wide, campanulate-convex, becoming broadly convex to nearly plane in age; surface moist or dry, glabrous, yellow to golden yellow or pale orange-yellow, fading in age, margin even; flesh white to whitish; odor not distinctive; taste bitter.

Gills: adnate to sinuate, close, pale yellow or yellowish white at first, becoming rust-spotted in age.

Stalk: 1–2⅜" (2.5–6 cm) long, ⅛–¼" (3–7 mm) thick, nearly equal or enlarged downward, dry, glabrous or nearly so, pale yellow to yellowish white, with a white tomentum over the base; partial veil fibrillose, white, not leaving a ring or sometimes leaving a faint annular zone.

Spore print: orange-brown.

Microscopic features: spores 6.5–10 x 4–5.5 µm, ellipsoid, lacking a germ pore, warted, ochraceous, dextrinoid.

Fruiting: solitary, scattered or in groups on decaying wood, wood chips, or sawdust; July–November; fairly common; widely distributed across North America.

Comments: *Gymnopilus sapineus* is very similar but it has a minutely scaly cap (use a hand lens) that often becomes rimose in age, a scanty yellowish partial veil, and flesh that usually has a pungent odor.

Dye notes:

no mordant	∘	gold
alum	·	gold
chrome	··	light beige
tin	···	brownish orange
copper	····	golden brown
iron	·····	greenish brown

Gymnopilus sapineus (Fries) Maire

Illus. p. 140

Cap: ¾–2¾" (2–7 cm) wide, hemispheric when young, becoming broadly convex; surface coated with minute scales, golden yellow to tawny, paler on the margin; flesh yellow; odor pungent or not distinctive; taste bitter or not distinctive.

Gills: attached, close, broad, yellow to orange-yellow when young, becoming brownish cinnamon to rusty yellow; edges minutely fringed.

Stalk: 1–2¾" (2.5–7 cm) long, ⅛–⅜" (3–10 mm) thick, nearly equal or tapered toward the base, yellowish, becoming brownish near the base, often hollow in age; partial veil present on the button stage, cortinate, sparse, yellowish, sometimes leaving a thin annular zone.

Spore print: rusty orange to rusty brown.

Microscopic features: spores 7–10 x 4–5.5 µm, elliptic, slightly roughened, lacking an apical pore, pale brown.

Fruiting: scattered or in groups on decaying wood and sawdust; July–October; fairly common; widely distributed in North America.

Comments: *Gymnopilus penetrans* is very similar but it has a glabrous cap, a white partial veil, and its flesh lacks a pungent odor.

Dye notes:

no mordant	∘	yellow
alum	·	yellow-orange
chrome	··	brownish orange
tin	···	dark orange
copper	····	golden brown
iron	·····	greenish brown

Gymnopilus ventricosus (Earle) Hesler

Illus. p. 141

Cap: 2⅜–10" (6–25 cm) wide, convex, becoming broadly convex to nearly plane, typically deeply depressed to funnel-shaped in age; surface moist or dry, fibrillose to glabrous, reddish brown to yellowish brown, fading in age, margin elevated at maturity, sometimes weakly appendiculate with yellowish fibills; flesh pale yellow; odor not distinctive; taste bitter or not distinctive.

Gills: attached to decurrent, close to crowded, broad, pale brown at first, becoming dark cinnamon-brown at maturity.

Stalk: 3½–8" (9–20 cm) long, ¾–2⅜" (2–6 cm) thick, tapered downward or sometimes nearly equal, dry, solid, fibrillose to glabrous, pale reddish brown, whitish near the apex, with a white basal mycelium; partial veil fibrillose, yellowish to pale brown, leaving a ragged superior ring.

Spore print: dark rusty brown.

Microscopic features: spores 7–9 x 4–5.5 μm, ellipsoid to ovoid, verruculose, lacking an apical pore, pale brown, slowly dextrinoid.

Fruiting: solitary, scattered or in groups on the ground, usually at the base of pines, December–February; occasional; California.

Dye notes:

no mordant	◦	yellow
alum	·	yellow-orange
chrome	··	brownish orange
tin	···	dark orange
copper	····	golden brown
iron	·····	greenish brown

Hebeloma mesophaeum (Persoon : Fries) Quélet

Illus. p. 141

Cap: ¾–2⅜" (2–6 cm) wide, convex, becoming broadly convex, often depressed at the center, sometimes with an umbo; margin inrolled at first, becoming decurved well into maturity, sometimes uplifted and wavy in age, typically rimmed with cortinate veil remnants; surface viscid, fibrillose, especially near the margin, reddish brown to orange-brown over the center, brownish yellow to yellowish tan toward the margin; flesh pale watery brown; odor not distinctive; taste radish-like then bitter.

Gills: sinuate to notched, close, whitish at first, becoming grayish brown at maturity; edges whitish and finely fringed in age.

Stalk: 1⅛–3½" (3–9 cm) long, ⅛–⅜" (3–10 mm) thick, nearly equal, dry, fibrillose-striate, white at first, becoming dull brown from the base upward in age; partial veil cortinate, pale yellow, soon stained brownish by falling spores, leaving veil remnants on the cap margin or a fibrous, superior annular zone.

Spore print: rusty brown.

Microscopic features: spores 8–11 x 4–7 μm, broadly elliptic, slightly roughened, pale brown.

Fruiting: scattered or in groups on soil or grassy areas, in conifer or hardwoods, often found under bushes and hedges in residential areas; April–November; fairly common; widely distributed in North America.

Dye notes:

no mordant	◦	none
alum	·	beige
chrome	··	beige
tin	···	light yellow
copper	····	beige
iron	·····	beige

Hygrophorus conicus (Fries) Fries Illus. p. 141

Cap: ¾–3½" (2–9 cm) wide, sharply conic to bell-shaped, usually with an umbo; surface smooth, slightly sticky when moist, otherwise dry, dark orange-red to red, orange, lighter orange near the margin or sometimes yellow overall, often with olive-green tints, quickly staining black when bruised or in age; flesh thin, fragile, colored like the cap, bruising black; odor and taste not distinctive.

Gills: free from the stalk, close, broad, waxy, light yellow to greenish orange, bruising black.

Stalk: ¾–4" (2–10 cm) long, ⅛–⅜" (3–10 mm) thick, equal, hollow, fragile, smooth, not sticky, often longitudinally striate or twisted-striate, yellow to yellow-orange, pale yellow near the base, staining black when bruised or in age; partial veil and ring absent.

Spore print: white.

Microscopic features: spores 8–14 x 5–7 µm, elliptic, smooth, hyaline, inamyloid.

Fruiting: solitary to scattered on the ground under conifers; July–September; occasional to fairly common; widely distributed in North America.

Comments: Also known as *Hygrocybe conica.*

Dye notes: *

no mordant	◦	light greenish brown
alum	·	light brown
chrome	··	light greenish brown
tin	···	olive
copper	····	light greenish brown
iron	·····	green-gray

Hypholoma aurantiacum (Cooke) Faus Illus. p. 141

Cap: ⅝–2⅜" (1.5–6 cm) wide, convex, becoming broadly umbonate to nearly plane in age; surface dry to slightly viscid, glabrous, bright scarlet to orange-red at first, fading to reddish orange or dull orange in age, sometimes with reddish brown tones; margin often rimmed with whitish partial veil remnants; flesh dingy whitish; odor and taste not distinctive.

Gills: close, attached or notched, often seceding in age, whitish to yellowish at first, becoming grayish brown and finally purple-brown to purple-black in age.

Stalk: ¾–3½" (2–9 cm) long, ⅛–⅜" (3–10 mm) thick, nearly equal or tapered slightly in either direction, dry, solid, streaked with longitudinal fibrills, white overall or with yellowish tints at the base, developing reddish orange stains on the lower portion in age or when handled; partial veil fibrillose, white, evanescent or leaving a sparse superior annular zone.

Spore print: purple-brown.

Microscopic features: spores 10–14 x 5–9 µm, elliptic, smooth, brown; pleurocystida present as chrysocystidia.

Fruiting: scattered or in groups on decaying wood chips, sawdust, humus, in lawns, gardens, compost areas, and on fallen eucalyptus seed pods; July–May; fairly common; California, distribution limits yet to be established.

Comments: This mushroom was formerly known as *Naematoloma aurantiacum.*

Dye notes:

no mordant	◦	yellow-beige
alum	·	light brownish yellow
chrome	··	brownish yellow
tin	···	gold
copper	····	light olive
iron	·····	beige

Hypholoma sublateritium (Fries) Quélet

Illus. p. 141

Cap: 1–4" (2.5–10 cm) wide, convex, becoming broadly convex to nearly flat; surface smooth, moist or dry, with scattered yellowish fibrils, brick-red with yellow-orange at or near the margin; flesh dull yellow to pale yellowish brown, thick, firm; odor not distinctive; taste mild or bitter.

Gills: attached, close, narrow, whitish to pale greenish yellow, becoming purplish gray to purple-brown at maturity; not staining when cut or bruised.

Stalk: 2–4" (5–10 cm) long, ¼–⅝" (6–15 mm) thick, equal, hollow in age, pale yellow to whitish above the ring, dull brown or grayish below, covered with reddish brown fibrils; partial veil fibrous to cortinate, leaving a sparse superior ring or annular zone.

Spore print: purple-brown.

Microscopic features: spores 6–7 x 3.5–4.5 μm, eliptical with an apical pore, smooth, pale brown.

Fruiting: in dense clusters or scattered on hardwood stumps or logs; August–October; common; eastern North America.

Comments: This mushroom was formerly known as *Naematoloma sublateritium.*

Dye notes:

no mordant	◦	yellowish beige
alum	·	light yellow
chrome	··	beige
tin	···	yellow
copper	····	gold
iron	·····	light greenish brown

Inocybe angustispora A. E. Bessette and Fatto

Illus. p. 141

Cap: ⅜–2" (1–5 cm) wide, convex, becoming broadly convex to nearly plane, not umbonate, sometimes shallowly depressed on the disc; surface dry, silky smooth, becoming appressed-fibrillose along the margin, ochraceous-tawny to ochraceous-brown or olive-brown, typically with grayish brown to fuscous tints over the disc, margin incurved at first, becoming decurved, even; flesh very thin, whitish to pale yellow, unchanging when exposed; odor and taste not distinctive.

Gills: adnate with a decurrent tooth, to sinuate, seceding in age, narrow, subdistant, pale yellow to greenish yellow at first, becoming dull yellow and finally dull brownish yellow, drying rusty brown.

Stalk: ¾–2" (2–5 cm) long, 1⁄16–¼" (1.5–6 mm) thick, nearly equal down to a slightly bulbous base, dry, solid at first, becoming hollow at maturity, longitudinally fibrillose, pale yellow at first, becoming ochraceous to dull ochraceous-tawny; partial veil sparse, yellowish, evanescent.

Spore print: dull brown.
Microscopic features: spores 9–14 x 3.2–4.4 μm, elongate-suboblong to subfusoid, smooth, with one or two large oil drops, ochraceous to brownish ochraceous.
Macrochemical tests: cap stains violaceous-fuscous then quickly mahogany-red with the application of KOH or NH_4OH, and is negative with $FeSO_4$; flesh stains purplish then dull brown with the application of KOH or NH_4OH, and slowly weakly olive with $FeSO_4$.
Fruiting: scattered or in groups on sand dunes under pine and oak; September–November; occasional to locally common; reported only from Cape Cod, Massachusetts and the Rome Sand Plains of central New York.
Comments: This species of *Inocybe* has most unusual spores that closely resemble those found in many boletes. Dried specimens mounted in KOH produce a leaching of reddish pigment.
Dye notes:

no mordant	◦	light pink
alum	·	light purplish pink
chrome	··	light purplish pink
tin	···	light golden brown
copper	····	light reddish brown
iron	·····	light brown

Leucocoprinus birnbaumii (Corda) Singer

Illus. p. 142

Cap: ¾–2⅜" (2–6 cm) wide, campanulate to broadly conic, typically with an umbo; surface dry, powdery or with tiny scales, bright to pale yellow, becoming pale yellow to whitish in age, margin distinctly striate to the disc; flesh very thin, whitish to pale yellow; odor and taste not distinctive.
Gills: free, crowded, whitish to pale yellow; edges fibrillose.
Stalk: 1½–4½" (4–11.5 cm) long, 1⁄16–¼" (1.5–6 mm) thick, enlarged downward or sometimes nearly equal, dry, smooth, or powdery, colored like the cap; partial veil fibrous-cottony, bright yellow, leaving a movable persistent or evanescent ring.
Spore print: white.
Microscopic features: spores 8–13 x 5–8 μm, elliptic, smooth, thick-walled, hyaline, dextrinoid.
Fruiting: scattered, in groups, or clusters on rich soils, wood chips used for landscaping, in greenhouses, and on soil in potted plants; July–October, year-round indoors; fairly common; widespread throughout the southern United States.
Comments: This mushroom is also known as *Lepiota lutea* (Bolton) Quélet.
Dye notes:

no mordant	◦	light beige
alum	·	beige
chrome	··	yellow-brown
tin	···	yellow-brown
copper	····	yellow-brown
iron	·····	gray

Omphalotus olivascens Bigelow, Miller, and Thiers Illus. p. 142

Cap: 2–10" (4–25 cm) wide, broadly convex, becoming nearly plane in age, sometimes shallowly depressed; surface dry, smooth, color variable, golden yellow to dull orange or brownish orange, usually with olive tones present, especially in age, margin incurved at first, becoming decurved, often wavy in age; flesh olivaceous to dull orange; odor and taste not distinctive.

Gills: decurrent, close to subdistant, olive to yellow-orange, often olive mottled with dull yellow.

Stalk: 1½–8¾" (4–22 cm) long, ⅜–2" (1–5 cm) thick, tapered downward or nearly equal, eccentric to central, dry, solid, glabrous or longitudinally fibrillose, olive to olive-yellow or dull yellow, typically fused at the base; partial veil and ring absent.

Spore print: whitish to yellowish.

Microscopic features: spores 6–8 x 6–7 μm, subglobose to elliptic, smooth, hyaline.

Macrochemical tests: flesh stains dark vinaceous with the application of KOH.

Fruiting: usually clustered or sometimes solitary on or near hardwood tree bases or stumps, sometimes attached to buried wood; September–April; fairly common; Pacific Coast.

Comments: The gills of fresh specimens are usually luminescent.

Dye notes:

no mordant	◦	gray
alum	·	gray-purple
chrome	··	olive
tin	···	blue-green
copper	····	blackish brown
iron	·····	olive

Paxillus atrotomentosus (Batsch) Fries Illus. p. 142

Cap: 1½–5⅞" (4–15 cm) wide, convex, becoming flat, sometimes depressed at the center; surface dry, felty to smooth, covered with matted hairs, dull olive-brown to rusty brown or yellowish brown to blackish brown; margin inrolled when young; flesh whitish, thick, tough, not staining when cut; odor and taste not distinctive.

Gills: decurrent, close, often forked or pore-like near the stalk, tan to yellow-brown or dull yellow, not staining when bruised.

Stalk: ¾–4" (2–10 cm) long, ⅜–1¼" (1–3 cm) thick, equal, eccentric to nearly lateral, solid, velvety with a covering of densely matted dark brown or blackish brown hairs, apex often lighter; partial veil and ring absent.

Spore print: dull yellow to pale brownish yellow.

Microscopic features: spores 5–7 x 3–4 μm, elliptic, smooth, hyaline to pale brown.

Fruiting: solitary, in groups or clusters on decaying conifer stumps and logs or partially buried wood; July–October; occasional to fairly common; northern north America and south along coastal mountains.

Dye notes:

no mordant	◦	brown
alum	·	dark purple
chrome	··	dark olive
tin	···	blackish blue
copper	····	blackish brown
iron	·····	dark olive

Best color results are obtained using a 6:5 ratio of mushroom to wool.

Paxillus involutus (Batsch) Fries

Illus. p. 142

Cap: 1⅝–4¾" (4–12 cm) wide, convex, becoming flat, often depressed on the disc; surface dry, smooth, somewhat sticky when moist, occasionally finely cracked in age, covered with matted hairs, dull brown, yellow-brown or red-brown, sometimes with olive tints; margin inrolled until maturity; flesh dull yellow to pale tan, bruising reddish brown when cut or bruised; odor and taste not distinctive.

Gills: decurrent, crowded, broad, forked and often pore-like near the stalk, tan to dull yellow or olive-yellow, staining reddish brown when bruised or in age.

Stalk: ¾–4" (2–10 cm) long, ¼–¾" (6–20 mm) thick, nearly equal or enlarged downward, solid, usually central, yellow-brown, often with darker brown stains, smooth; partial veil and ring absent.

Spore print: pale to dark yellow-brown.

Microscopic features: spores 7–9 x 4–6 μm, elliptic, smooth, pale brown.

Fruiting: solitary, scattered or in groups on the ground or on decaying wood in conifer or mixed woods; July–November; fairly common; widely distributed across North America.

Dye notes:

no mordant	∘	beige
alum	·	pinkish beige
chrome	··	light pinkish brown
tin	···	light golden brown
copper	····	light greenish brown
iron	·····	light grayish brown

Paxillus panuoides Fries

Illus. p. 142

Cap: 1–4⅜" (2.5–11 cm) wide, fan- to petal-shaped; surface dry, smooth to felty, olive-yellow to yellow-brown; margin incurved when young, becoming uplifted, thin and wavy at maturity; flesh whitish to pale cream; odor and taste not distinctive or taste somewhat bitter.

Gills: thin, radiating from the point of attachment to the substrate, sometimes forked or anastomosing, occasionally crossveined, often conspicuously wavy and corrugated but sometimes straight, pale yellow to pale yellow-orange, easily separated from the cap.

Stalk: absent or rudimentary.

Spore print: yellowish.

Microscopic features: spores 4–6 x 3–4 μm, elliptic, smooth, hyaline, weakly amyloid, not dextrinoid.

Fruiting: scattered or in overlapping clusters on decaying conifer wood; May–November; occasional; widely distributed across North America.

Dye notes:

no mordant	∘	light brown
alum	·	purple-gray
chrome	··	greenish brown
tin	···	olive
copper	····	greenish brown
iron	·····	olive

Pholiota albocrenulata (Peck) Saccardo

Illus. p. 142

Cap: 1–4¾" (2.5–12 cm) wide, obtuse to broadly conic or convex, becoming nearly plane at maturity, often with a low broad umbo; surface glutinous to viscid, orange-fulvous to deep ferruginous when fresh, becoming dark vinaceous-brown in age, with brown fibrillose scales; margin incurved at first usually with brown scales; flesh whitish; odor not distinctive; taste not distinctive or somewhat bitter.

Gills: adnate to subdecurrent or sinuate and with a decurrent tooth, close, broad, whitish at first, becoming grayish then rusty brown; edges crenulate, usually beaded with white drops when fresh.

Stalk: 1⅛–6" (3–15 cm) long, ¼–⅝" (5–16 mm) thick, nearly equal overall, dry, becoming hollow in age, dark brown and scaly below the ring, whitish to grayish and pruinose above; partial veil brownish and fibrillose-scaly, usually leaving a conspicuous superior ring.

Spore print: cinnamon-brown.

Microscopic features: spores 10–17 x 5.5–8 µm, subfusoid, smooth, brown.

Fruiting: solitary, in groups, or small clusters on decaying hardwood trunks, stumps, and logs, especially maple, sometimes on poplar and pine; July–October; occasional; eastern Canada south to North Carolina, west to Michigan and New Mexico.

Dye notes:

no mordant	◦	none
alum	·	light yellow
chrome	··	light brownish yellow
tin	···	yellow
copper	····	greenish yellow
iron	·····	beige

Pholiota aurivella (Fries) Kummer

Illus. p. 143

Cap: 1½–6⅜" (4–16 cm) wide, campanulate to convex, often broadly umbonate; surface viscid to glutinous, ochraceous-orange to tawny, darkening in age, covered with large flattened scales that sometimes disappear at maturity; margin incurved at first, becoming decurved at maturity; flesh yellow; odor and taste not distinctive.

Gills: adnate to sinuate, close, broad, pale yellow at first, becoming rusty brown at maturity.

Stalk: 2–3⅛" (5–8 cm) long, ¼–⅝" (5–15 mm) thick, nearly equal overall, dry, solid, floccose above the ring, fibrillose below and becoming conspicuously scaly downward, yellowish to yellowish brown; partial veil whitish to pale yellow leaving a fibrillose superior ring that is often evanescent.

Spore print: dull brown.

Microscopic features: spores 7–11 x 4.5–6 µm, broadly elliptic to broadly oblong, smooth, with a distinct apical pore, brownish.

Fruiting: in clusters on trunks, stumps, and logs of conifers or hardwoods; August–November; fairly common; widely distributed throughout North America.

Dye notes:

no mordant	◦	beige
alum	·	light yellow
chrome	··	light brown
tin	···	orange-yellow
copper	····	yellow-brown
iron	·····	light brown

Pholiota flammans (Fries) Kummer Illus. p. 143

Cap: 1¼–4" (3–10 cm) wide, sticky to slippery, smooth, bright yellow to orangish yellow or yellowish orange only at the center, with curved, fibrous scales; flesh yellow; odor and taste not distinctive.

Gills: attached and sharply notched, close to crowded, rather broad, bright yellow at first, soon staining brown on the edges where bruised; partial veil thin, yellow, fibrous to cortinate, usually leaving only a zone of fibers but sometimes an almost membranous ring on the upper stalk.

Stalk: dry, bright yellow, becoming orangish yellow near the base in age, densely covered with cottony-fibrous scales below the annular zone.

Spore print: rusty brown.

Microscopic features: spores 4–5 x 2.5–3 µm, oblong to elliptic, usually with a distinct apiculus, apical pore not evident, brownish.

Fruiting: solitary or more typically in small clusters on coniferous logs and stumps; August–October; occasional; eastern Canada south to North Carolina and Tennessee, west to the Pacific Northwest.

Dye notes:

no mordant	∘	yellow
alum	·	brownish orange
chrome	··	brownish orange
tin	···	dark orange
copper	····	brown
iron	·····	olive

Pholiota malicola* var. *macropoda Smith and Hesler Illus. p. 143

Cap: 1¼–5" (3–15 cm) wide, convex to nearly flat, moist to sticky or slippery at first but soon dry, smooth, yellow to orangish yellow, sometimes with a greenish tinge, decorated at most with faint whitish to buff fibers near the opaque margin; flesh yellowish, rather thick; odor faintly fragrant (often like green corn), taste not distinctive.

Gills: attached or notched, close, narrow to moderately broad, yellowish at first, becoming pale rusty brown in age, sometimes slowly staining orange where bruised, edges even (not white-fringed); partial veil whitish to buff, fibrous to cortinate, usually leaving a slight zone of fibers on the upper stalk and cap margin.

Stalk: 1½–7" (4–18 cm) long, ⅛–1" (4–25 mm) thick, sometimes tapered toward the base, dry, whitish to yellowish and silky at the top, lower portion fibrous to striate, becoming dark rusty brown from the base upward, with only a slight zone of fibers on the upper stalk.

Spore print: brown.

Microscopic features: spores 7.5–11 x 4.5–5.5 µm, with a distinct apical pore but apex not truncate, pale brownish, somewhat dextrinoid.

Fruiting: in clusters, usually at the base of deciduous or coniferous trees or stumps but sometimes on woody debris or soil; August–November; occasional; widely distributed in North America.

Dye notes:

no mordant	∘	beige
alum	·	yellow-beige
chrome	··	beige
tin	···	gold
copper	····	greenish beige
iron	·····	beige

Pholiota squarrosa (Fries) Kummer

Illus. p. 27

Cap: 1¼–5" (3–12.5 cm) wide, cuticle entirely broken up into dry, tan to pinkish tan or brownish scales; margin usually decorated with yellowish to tan remnants from the partial veil at maturity; flesh pale yellow, odor usually strong of garlic, in some collections reportedly absent or more similar to onions; taste unpleasant or not distinctive.

Gills: attached, usually with fine decurrent lines, close to crowded, moderately narrow; pale yellow at first, soon developing distinct green tones, finally dirty rusty brown but often with greenish tones remaining evident; covered at first by a fibrous-membranous yellowish or tan partial veil.

Stalk: 1½–5" (4–12.5 cm) long, ⅛–⅝" (4–15 mm) thick, sometimes tapered toward the base; dry, scaly like the cap; often with a somewhat membranous ring.

Spore print: brown.

Microscopic features: spores 5–8 x 3.5–4.5 μm, elliptic to oval, with a distinct apical pore but not truncate, brownish, weakly dextrinoid.

Fruiting: usually in large clusters on or at the base of deciduous or coniferous trees, stumps or logs; July–November; occasional to common; widely distributed in North America.

Comments: Compare with *Pholiota squarrosoides,* which has a sticky cap and its flesh lacks a garlic-like odor.

Dye notes:

no mordant	◦	yellow-beige
alum	·	yellow-beige
chrome	··	beige
tin	···	gold
copper	····	greenish beige
iron	·····	beige

Pholiota squarrosoides (Peck) Saccardo

Illus. p. 143

Cap: 1–4" (2.5–10 cm) wide, obtuse to convex, becoming broadly convex to nearly plane, sometimes with an umbo; surface sticky when fresh, whitish at first, soon becoming orangish to brownish beneath a dense covering of scales; scales dry, erect, pointed, tawny or tan to pale brownish; flesh thick, whitish; odor and taste not distinctive.

Gills: notched or attached, close to crowded, moderately broad, whitish at first, becoming dull rusty brown in age.

Stalk: 2–6" (5–15.5 cm) long, ¼–⅝" (5–15 mm) thick, nearly equal or slightly enlarged near the base, dry, solid, whitish and silky above the ring, sheathed below with a dense layer of dry, ochre-tawny scales; partial veil cottony-fibrous to almost membranous, whitish, leaving a torn, cottony-fibrous, sometimes evanescent ring on the upper stalk and remnants on the cap margin.

Spore print: brown.

Microscopic features: spores 4–6 x 2.5–3.5 μm, elliptic to oval, with a slight apiculus, lacking a distinct apical pore, smooth, yellowish.

Fruiting: in dense clusters on decaying hardwoods; July–October; fairly common; widely distributed in North America.

Comments: *Pholiota squarrosa* is very similar but it has a dry, not sticky, cap surface, and its flesh has a weak to strong garlic-like odor.

Dye notes:

no mordant	∘	yellow
alum	·	light golden brown
chrome	··	light golden brown
tin	···	gold
copper	····	light golden brown
iron	·····	light greenish brown

Pholiota velaglutinosa A. H. Smith and Hesler

Illus. p. 143

Cap: 1⅛–2⅜" (3–6 cm) wide, convex, becoming broadly convex to nearly plane; surface glutinous to viscid when fresh, appearing streaked beneath the gluten, vinaceous-brown to pale reddish brown, margin sometimes elevated and wavy in age, typically appendiculate with the remains of the glutinous partial veil; flesh greenish yellow, becoming whitish in age; odor and taste not distinctive.

Gills: attached and usually with a decurrent tooth, close, moderately broad, pale pinkish brown at first, becoming darker brown at maturity.

Stalk: 1⅛–2¾" (3–7 cm) long, ⅛–5⁄16" (3–8 mm) thick, nearly equal, dry to slightly viscid, hollow, silky and greenish yellow above the ring, with fibrillose patches or concentric zones below; partial veil glutinous; ring superior, glutinous, evanescent.

Spore print: dark brown.

Microscopic features: spores 6–8 x 3.5–4.5 μm, elliptic to broadly elliptic, with a minute apical pore, smooth, dull cinnamon.

Fruiting: scattered or in groups on wood chips and other organic debris under conifers, especially pines; October–February; fairly common; California and Oregon.

Dye notes:

no mordant	∘	light yellow
alum	·	light orange
chrome	··	light yellow-brown
tin	···	orange
copper	····	golden brown
iron	·····	greenish brown

Psathyrella velutina (Fries) Singer

Illus. p. 143

Cap: ¾–4¾" (2–12 cm) wide, oval to hemispheric when young, becoming convex and finally plane, often with an umbo; surface covered with a dense layer of tiny silky flattened fibers, many of which aggregate into tiny scales, orange-brown to dark yellow-brown, darkest on the disc; margin often rimmed with flaps of partial veil; flesh yellowish brown; odor and taste not distinctive.

Gills: attached, close, pale to dark brown, mottled; edges white, often beaded with moisture drops when fresh.

Stalk: 1⅛–4¾" (3–12 cm) long, ⅛–⅝" (3–16 mm) thick, equal, pale yellowish brown with dull orange-brown fibers and scales below the ring, smooth and whitish above; partial veil cottony-fibrous, leaving a superior thin zone of fibrils.

Spore print: blackish brown.

Microscopic features: spores 8–12 x 6–8 μm, elliptic, smooth, with an apical pore, pale brown.

Macrochemical tests: flesh stains dark rusty brown with the application of KOH.
Fruiting: solitary, scattered or in small clusters in grassy areas and organic debris; July–October; fairly common; widely distributed in North America.
Comments: also known as *Lacrymaria velutina*.
Dye notes:

no mordant	◦	pinkish beige
alum	·	light pinkish brown
chrome	··	light pinkish brown
tin	···	pinkish brown
copper	····	light brown
iron	·····	pinkish beige

Russula ventricosipes Peck

Illus. p. 27

Cap: 2–5½" (5–14 cm) wide, convex, becoming nearly plane; surface viscid when moist, often coated with sand, needle litter and debris, tawny-yellow to dull brown; margin typically tuberculate-striate; flesh whitish to pale yellow; odor weak or strong of marzipan or bitter almonds, or somewhat foetid; taste weakly to strongly acrid.
Gills: attached, close, often forked near the stalk, dull white to creamy yellow.
Stalk: ¾–4" (2–10 cm) long, ⅜–1½" (1–4 cm) thick, nearly equal down to a tapered base, reddish pruinose overall or at least near the base, ground color whitish.
Spore print: dark cream.
Microscopic features: spores 7–10 x 4–6 μm, lacrymoid, with very tiny projections, appearing nearly smooth, hyaline, amyloid.
Fruiting: solitary, scattered or in groups, often partially buried in sandy soil near pines; July–October; fairly common; widespread in the northern United States and Canada.
Dye notes:

no mordant	◦	light brownish orange
alum	·	light brownish orange
chrome	··	light brownish orange
tin	···	light brownish orange
copper	····	light yellow-brown
iron	·····	light brownish orange

Stropharia ambigua (Peck) Zeller

Illus. p. 144

Cap: 1⅛–5½" (3–14 cm) wide, obtuse to convex, becoming broadly convex to nearly plane in age, margin appendiculate with cottony white remnants; surface viscid when fresh, smooth, yellow to yellowish buff or sometimes paler; flesh white; odor and taste not distinctive.
Gills: adnate or seceding, close, whitish at first, becoming grayish to purplish brown at maturity.
Stalk: 2–7" (5–18 cm) long, ¼–¾" (6–20 mm) thick, nearly equal or slightly enlarged downward, dry, usually hollow in age, white and silky near the apex, fibrillose or sheathed below with soft cottony white scales, sometimes yellowish on the lower portion, usually with numerous white rhizomorphs at the base; partial veil white, cottony, usually not forming a ring.
Spore print: purplish black.

Microscopic features: spores 11–14 x 6–8 µm, elliptic, smooth, purplish brown; pleurocystidia present as chrysocystidia.

Fruiting: solitary, scattered, or in groups on the ground or in rich humus under conifers or hardwoods; October–April; fairly common; Pacific Coast.

Dye notes: *

no mordant	∘	light greenish gray
alum	·	greenish gray
chrome	··	greenish gray
tin	···	light greenish brown
copper	····	light green
iron	·····	greenish gray

Tricholoma vaccinum (Persoon : Fries) Kummer

Illus. p. 144

Cap: 1–3⅛" (2.5–8 cm) wide, conic to convex when young, becoming broadly convex to nearly plane, with an umbo; surface coated with small fibrous scales, typically not coarsely cracked on the disc at maturity; fibrous scales reddish brown on a white ground color; margin inrolled and cottony-fibrous at first, becoming expanded and remaining cottony-fibrous and somewhat thickened in age; flesh white, developing reddish tinges when cut.

Gills: notched to sinuate, close, whitish buff when young, staining reddish brown when bruised or in age.

Stalk: 1–3⅛" (2.5–8 cm) long, ⅜–⅝" (1–1.6 cm) thick, nearly equal or slightly enlarged downward, hollow at maturity, fibrillose, reddish brown or paler; partial veil cottony-fibrous, not leaving a ring.

Spore print: white.

Microscopic features: spores 5.5–7 x 4–5 µm, oval to elliptic, smooth, hyaline.

Fruiting: scattered, in groups or clusters under conifers; July–November; occasional to fairly common; widely distributed in North America.

Dye notes:

no mordant	∘	beige
alum	·	beige
chrome	··	dark beige
tin	···	brownish yellow
copper	····	greenish brown
iron	·····	beige

Tricholomopsis rutilans (Schaeffer : Fries) Singer

Illus. p. 144

Cap: 2–4" (5–10 cm) wide, convex, becoming nearly plane in age; surface dry, covered with red to purplish red scales and fibers over a yellowish ground color; flesh pale yellow; odor and taste not distinctive.

Gills: attached or notched, close, yellow, with numerous tiers of lamellulae.

Stalk: 2–4⅜" (5–11 cm) long, ⅜–1" (1–2.5 cm) thick, nearly equal, frequently curved, dry, coated with red to purplish red scales and fibers over a yellowish ground color, often hollow in age.

Spore print: white.

Microscopic features: spores 5–7 x 3–5 µm, elliptic, smooth, hyaline.

Fruiting: scattered or in groups on decaying conifer wood, especially pine, and on rich humus in conifer woods; May–November; occasional; widely distributed in North America.

Dye notes: *

no mordant	∘	brownish yellow
alum	·	brown
chrome	··	brown
tin	···	brownish yellow
copper	····	dark brown
iron	·····	brown-black

Hypomyces

Hypomyces species are fungi that parasitize and disfigure other fungi. They are also known as hyperparasites. *Hypomyces* belong to the Pyrenomycetes, a class of Ascomycetes commonly called the Flask Fungi. They produce flask-shaped to rounded sexual structures called perithecia in which asci produce ascospores. The perithecia are often partially embedded in the host tissue, and their protruding necks are responsible for the sandpaper-like texture which covers some hosts.

Hypomyces lactifluorum (Schweinitz) Tulasne Illus. p. 31

Fruiting body: orange to reddish orange, sometimes with whitish areas, roughened like sandpaper, growing over the surface of funnel-shaped to irregular caps, stalks and deformed gills of host mushrooms; parasitized caps are typically dense, often partially buried in conifer debris, measure 2–7⅞" (5–20cm) wide, and are white and firm within.

Microscopic features: spores 35–40 x 4.5–7 μm, spindle-shaped, two-celled, prominently warted, hyaline.

Fruiting: partially imbedded in species of *Lactarius* and *Russula* which may be solitary, scattered or in groups on the ground in woods, usually under conifers; July–November; infrequent to fairly common; widely distributed across North America.

Dye notes:

no mordant	∘	pinkish orange
alum	·	pinkish orange
chrome	··	orange-pink
tin	···	orange
copper	····	dark orange-pink
iron	·····	dark orange-pink

The following colors were obtained when the pH was increased to 8–9 (see photo p. 16)

no mordant	∘	orange-pink
alum	·	orange-pink
chrome	··	purple
tin	···	orange-pink
copper	····	brown
iron	·····	brownish pink

Polypores

Members of this very large group of fungi form fruiting bodies with small cylindric tubes on the underside of the cap in which spores are produced. Spores are discharged through a tiny mouth-like opening at the end of each tube called a pore. Each fruiting body forms many tubes, each with a pore, which accounts for the name polypore. Several other common names have been used to describe various species in this diverse group including bracket fungi, shelf fungi, and conks. Some polypores have a central to eccentric or lateral stalk while others are stalkless. Most species grow on wood, but a few grow on soil or humus.

While many polypores are hard and woody or corky to leathery, some are fleshy to fibrous. The tube layer of a polypore usually does not separate cleanly and easily from the supporting cap tissue. A similar group called boletes resembles polypores that grow on the ground and also produce their spores in tubes. Most boletes grow on the ground, are soft and fleshy and their tube layers are usually cleanly and easily separated from the supporting cap tissue. Much of the information provided in this section is based on the descriptions of Gilbertson and Ryvarden (1986, 1987).

For best color results when dying with polypores, bring the pH up to 8 or 9 after simmering the mushrooms for ten minutes. *The one exception to this recommendation is Phaeolus schweinitzii.*

Amylocystis lapponica (Romell) Singer Illus. p. 144

Fruiting body: 2–6" (5–15 cm) wide, annual, rounded to fan- or shell-shaped, stalkless; upper surface tomentose to hispid, azonate, pale buff at first, becoming dark reddish brown with age, bruising, or drying; margin usually rounded.

Flesh: up to ¾" (2 cm) thick, corky to fibrous-tough, pale buff or slightly darker, azonate; odor usually strong of iodine when fresh.

Pore surface: white when fresh, becoming dark reddish brown with age, bruising, or drying; pores angular, 3–4 per mm.

Spore print: white.

Microscopic features: spores 8–11 x 2.5–3.5 µm, cylindric, smooth, hyaline; cystidia amyloid.

Fruiting: solitary or in overlapping, often fused clusters on decaying conifer wood; July–October; uncommon; northeastern and western North America.

Comments: *Oligoporus fragilis* is very similar but has much smaller spores, lacks cystidia, and does not have a distinctive odor when fresh.

Dye notes:

no mordant	∘	pinkish beige
alum	·	pinkish beige
chrome	··	light brown
tin	···	reddish brown
copper	····	golden brown
iron	·····	light reddish brown

Boletopsis subsquamosa (Fries) Kotlaba and Pouzar

Illus. p. 144

Cap: 2–5½" (5–14 cm) wide, circular, convex to broadly convex, usually somewhat depressed; surface dry, smooth, slightly fibrillose-scaly over the disc in age; color variable, dingy white, grayish, brownish or black, darkening when bruised or in age; margin slightly inrolled at first, becoming elevated, wavy and sometimes furrowed or split in age.

Flesh: firm, thick, white to pale grayish; odor not distinctive; taste somewhat bitter, becoming fragrant or spicy when dry.

Pore surface: subdecurrent, white at first, becoming grayish or pale brownish when dry; pores circular, 1–3 per mm.

Stalk: 1⅜–3⅛" (3–8 cm) long, ¾–1⅛" (2–3 cm) thick, central to slightly eccentric, nearly equal, fibrillose-scaly, grayish to olive-brown, solid.

Spore print: whitish to pale brown.

Microscopic features: spores 5–7 x 4–5 µm, angular and irregular, warted, hyaline.

Fruiting: solitary, scattered or in groups on the ground, usually partially buried in needle litter under conifers, occasionally under hardwoods; September–November; occasional to fairly common; widely distributed in North America.

Comments: This polypore resembles a bolete but the tube layer does not cleanly separate from the cap, the flesh is too tough and the spores are not typical of boletes.

Dye notes:

no mordant	∘	dark green
alum	·	black
chrome	··	black
tin	···	black
copper	····	dark green
iron	·····	black

Daedalea quercina Fries

Illus. p. 144

Cap: 2–8" (5–20.5 cm) wide, semicircular to kidney-shaped, stalkless, plane to slightly convex, leathery to corky or woody; surface felted to somewhat velvety when young, becoming smooth then cracked or furrowed in age, often concentrically zoned; color variable, usually brownish yellow to brownish orange, tan, brown or black; margin whitish and blunt.

Flesh: up to ⅜" (1 cm) thick, fibrous-tough, dull white to pale brown.

Pore surface: whitish to pale yellow-brown or grayish brown, conspicuously labyrinthine, occasionally with elongated pores near the margin; fibrous-tough.

Spore print: white.

Microscopic features: spores 5–6 x 2–3.5 µm, cylindric, smooth, hyaline.

Fruiting: solitary or in groups on decaying hardwoods, especially oak; year-round; occasional; throughout eastern North America.

Comments: *Cerrena unicolor* has a smaller cap, up to 3⅛" (8 cm) wide, with a dense layer of short stiff hairs, is variably colored and often green when coated with algae, with a white to gray labyrinthine pore surface. *Schizopora paradoxa* is a white to creamy white or grayish brown flattened spreading mass, with a labyrinthine pore surface, which grows on decaying hardwood logs and branches. *Daedaleopsis confragosa* is smaller and thinner.

Dye notes:

no mordant	◦	none
alum	·	none
chrome	··	beige
tin	···	beige
copper	····	light brown
iron	·····	beige

Echinodontium tinctorium Ellis and Everhart

Illus. p. 145

Fruiting body: 4¾–16" (12–40 cm) wide, hoof-shaped to semicircular or irregular, convex, stalkless; surface matted tomentose at first, soon becoming hard and crusty, cracking radially and concentrically into rectangular or irregular blocks and sometimes exposing bright orange to reddish orange flesh in the cracks, sulcate, dark dull brown when young, soon becoming blackish; margin blunt, roughened, dark olive-brown to blackish.

Flesh: up to 2" (5 cm) thick at the base, zoned; upper portion hard, crusty, and blackish; lower portion fibrous-tough and bright orange to reddish orange or brick-red.

Pore surface: at first irregularly poroid, soon forming flattened to cylindrical or irregular teeth, buff to pinkish buff when producing spores, becoming dull grayish brown to blackish in age, sometimes with bright orange to reddish orange flesh showing when teeth are broken; teeth up to 1⅛" (3 cm) long.

Spore print: white.

Microscopic features: spores 6–8 x 4–6 μm, minutely echinulate, smooth, hyaline.

Fruiting: solitary or in groups on decaying conifers, especially fir and hemlock; year-round, perennial; occasional to fairly common; western North America from Alaska south to California and New Mexico.

Dye notes:

no mordant	◦	light pinkish orange
alum	·	orange-red
chrome	··	purple-red
tin	···	orange-red
copper	····	pinkish brown
iron	·····	grayish purple

Fistulina hepatica Schaeffer : Fries

Illus. p. 145

Cap: 2¾–10" (7–25.5 cm) wide, fan- to spoon-shaped; surface smooth to velvety, gelatinous, often sticky to slimy; reddish orange to pinkish red or dark red to purplish brown; often exuding a red juice when squeezed; margin rounded or sharp, often wavy or lobed.

Flesh: ¾–2" (2–5 cm) thick, fleshy and juicy when fresh, becoming fibrous in age, dingy white to pinkish or reddish, zoned with darker and paler areas, slowly darkening when exposed; taste sour to acidic.

Pore surface: whitish to pinkish yellow, becoming reddish brown in age or when bruised; pores circular, 1–3 per mm; tubes crowded but distinctly separate when viewed with a hand lens.

Stalk: up to 3⅛" (8 cm) long, lateral to eccentric or sometimes absent, colored like the cap.
Spore print: pinkish salmon.
Microscopic features: spores 4–6 x 2.5–4 μm, oval to tear-shaped, smooth, hyaline.
Fruiting: solitary or in groups on oak trunks and stumps; July–October; infrequent; widely distributed in North America.
Dye notes:

no mordant	∘	beige
alum	·	beige
chrome	··	beige
tin	···	brown
copper	····	greenish brown
iron	·····	grayish brown

Fomes fasciatus (Swartz : Fries) M. C. Cooke

Illus. p. 145

Fruiting body: 2¾–7" (7–18 cm) wide, hoof- to fan-shaped or semicircular, convex, stalkless; surface finely tomentose and slightly roughened when young, becoming hard and nearly smooth at maturity, concentrically sulcate, typically zonate, grayish with concentric zones of reddish brown and grayish brown, often darker brown to blackish brown in age; margin somewhat sharp, curved.
Flesh: up to 1½" (4 cm) thick at the base, hard and crusty near the upper surface, fibrous to granular and corky below, golden brown.
Pore surface: pale brown at first, becoming dark grayish brown at maturity; pores circular, 4–5 per mm.
Spore print: white.
Microscopic features: spores 10–14 x 4–5 μm, cylindric, smooth, hyaline.
Fruiting: solitary, in groups or overlapping clusters on decaying hardwoods; year-round, perennial; fairly common; North Carolina south to Florida, west to Arizona.
Dye notes:

no mordant	∘	beige
alum	·	golden brown
chrome	··	yellow-brown
tin	···	golden brown
copper	····	light brown
iron	·····	grayish brown

Fomes fomentarius (Linnaeus : Fries) Kickx

Illus. p. 28

Cap: 2⅜–8" (6–20.5 cm) wide, hoof-shaped stalkless, woody; surface concentrically furrowed and zoned, hard, thick, crusty, thickened at the central point of attachment, finely cracked and roughened or smooth, pale to dark gray or sometimes pale to dark brown; margin blunt, extending beyond the pore surface.
Flesh: up to 1⅛" (3 cm) thick, fibrous-tough to woody, yellowish brown.
Pore surface: depressed, pale brown; pores circular, 3–5 per mm.
Spore print: white.
Microscopic features: spores 12–20 x 4–7 μm, cylindric, smooth, hyaline.
Fruiting: solitary, in groups or clusters on decaying hardwood; year-round, perennial; common; widely distributed across northern North America, south to North Carolina and Texas.

Dye notes:

no mordant	◦	light beige
alum	·	light golden brown
chrome	··	light golden brown
tin	···	light golden brown
copper	····	light greenish brown
iron	·····	olive

Ganoderma applanatum (Persoon) Patouillard

Illus. p. 145

Cap: 2–26" (5–65 cm) wide, shelf-like to somewhat hoof-shaped, stalkless, woody; surface hard, thick, crusty, concentrically furrowed, thickened at the central point of attachment, finely cracked and roughened, gray to grayish black or brown, dull; margin thin, often white.

Flesh: up to 2⅜" (6 cm) thick, corky to woody, brown.

Pore surface: white, staining brown when bruised; pores circular, 4–6 per mm.

Spore print: brown.

Microscopic features: spores 7–11 x 5–7.5 µm, broadly elliptic, truncate, with a thick double wall, pale brown.

Fruiting: solitary, scattered or in overlapping clusters on decaying wood, especially hardwood; year-round, perennial; common; throughout North America.

Dye notes:

no mordant	◦	beige
alum	·	golden brown
chrome	··	light brown
tin	···	brown
copper	····	golden brown
iron	·····	grayish brown

Ganoderma curtisii (Berkeley) Murrill

Illus. p. 145

Cap: 1⅛–8" (3–20 cm) wide, kidney- to fan-shaped, convex, corky to soft-corky; surface covered with a thin crust or varnish, zonate to furrowed, glabrous, bright ochraceous at first, becoming partly dull red to brick red and finally dull red overall in age; margin typically obtuse.

Flesh: up to ⅝" (1.5 cm) thick, soft to corky, whitish on the upper portion, brownish below.

Pore surface: white to brownish or tinged yellow, rapidly staining brown when bruised; pores circular to subcircular, 4–5 per mm.

Stalk: 1½–4" (4–10 cm) long, ¼–1" (7–25 mm) thick, lateral or subcentral, covered with a thin crust or varnish and colored like the cap, dry, solid, glabrous.

Spore print: brown.

Microscopic features: spores 9–13 x 5–7 µm, ovoid with a truncate apex and a thick wall, smooth, pale brown.

Fruiting: solitary or in groups on decaying stumps or trunks of hardwoods or attached to buried roots, May–January or sometimes year-round; fairly common; widely distributed in the eastern United States.

Comments: *Ganoderma lucidum* is similar but lacks the bright ochraceous color on young growing specimens, or has ochraceous tones only on the margin, and usually has a short stalk. Some authors consider *Ganoderma curtisii* and *Ganoderma lucidum* to be synonyms.

Dye notes:

no mordant	∘	beige
alum	·	golden brown
chrome	··	light golden brown
tin	···	brownish gold
copper	····	brown
iron	·····	grayish beige

Ganoderma tsugae Murrill

Illus. p. 145

Cap: 2⅜–12" (6–31 cm) wide, fan- to kidney-shaped; soft and corky when fresh, covered with a thin crust; surface smooth to wrinkled, shiny, appearing varnished or dull and powdery when covered with spores, concentrically zoned and shallowly furrowed; brownish red to mahagony near the center or overall, brownish orange to reddish orange outward and bright whitish on the margin or rarely blue to bluish green.

Flesh: up to 1⅛" (3 cm) thick, soft and corky to fibrous-tough, whitish.

Pore surface: white to creamy white, becoming brown in age or when bruised; pores circular to angular, 4–6 per mm.

Stalk: 1⅛–6" (3–15.5 cm) long, ⅜–1½" (1–4 cm) thick, typically lateral but sometimes eccentric to central or absent, shiny, appearing varnished, brownish red to mahagony or blackish brown.

Spore print: brown.

Microscopic features: spores 9–11 x 6–8 μm, elliptic, truncate, with a thick double wall, appearing rough, pale brown.

Fruiting: solitary or in groups on decaying conifer wood, especially hemlock; May–December; fairly common; eastern Canada south to North Carolina, west to the Midwest.

Comments: *Ganoderma lucidum* has a dark reddish brown cap with a creamy white margin and grows on decaying hardwoods, especially maple.

Dye notes:

no mordant	∘	beige
alum	·	pinkish brown
chrome	··	light brown
tin	···	light brown
copper	····	light brown
iron	·····	beige

Gloeophyllum sepiarium (Fries) Karsten

Illus. p. 146

Cap: 1–4" (2.5–10 cm) wide, semicircular to kidney-shaped, flat or slightly convex, stalkless, fibrous-tough; surface covered with short stiff hairs, becoming matted and felty or nearly smooth in age, with distinct concentric zones and furrows, bright yellowish red to reddish brown; margin whitish to orange-yellow or brownish yellow, uneven, with tufts of tiny hairs.

Flesh: up to ¼" (6 mm) thick, fibrous-tough, yellow-brown to rusty brown.
Pore surface: golden brown to rusty brown, gill-like to labyrinthine, often with both and sometimes with elongated pores; pores 1–2 per mm.
Spore print: white.
Microscopic features: spores 9–13 x 3–5 μm, cylindric, smooth, hyaline.
Macrochemical tests: flesh stains black with the application of KOH.
Fruiting: solitary, in groups or rosette-like clusters on decaying wood, usually conifer; year-round; common; widely distributed in North America.
Comments: *Lenzites betulina* has white flesh and usually grows on decaying hardwood. *Gloeophyllum trabeum* has crowded gills and narrow pores, up to 4 per mm along the margin.
Dye notes:

no mordant	∘	pinkish beige
alum	·	pinkish beige
chrome	··	light brown
tin	···	brownish gold
copper	····	light brown
iron	·····	light brown

Hapalopilus nidulans (Fries) Karsten

Illus. p. 28

Fruiting body: 1–4¾" (2.5–12 cm) wide, fan-shaped to semicircular, convex, stalkless, soft and watery when fresh, becoming corky to brittle when dry; surface coated with tiny matted hairs, becoming smooth in age, often with one or more shallow concentric furrows, dull brownish orange to cinnamon; margin sharp, curved.
Flesh: up to 1⅛" (3 cm) thick at the base, soft and watery when fresh, pale cinnamon.
Pore surface: ochraceous to cinnamon-brown; pores angular, 2–4 per mm.
Spore print: white.
Microscopic features: spores 3.5–5 x 2–3 μm, elliptic to cylindric, smooth, hyaline.
Macrochemical tests: all parts instantly stain bright violet with the application of KOH (see illus., p. 28).
Fruiting: solitary, in groups or overlapping clusters on decaying hardwood; June–November; fairly common in eastern and southwestern North America, occasional to rare in the northwest.
Dye notes:

no mordant	∘	light purple
alum	·	purple
chrome	··	grayish purple
tin	···	dark purple
copper	····	reddish brown
iron	·····	dark gray

One of the few mushrooms to produce purple, *Hapalopilus nidulans* is a very strong dyer requiring a relatively low mushroom:wool ratio to obtain excellent color results. Experiment with proportions as low as 1:5, mushroom to wool. Be certain to use successive afterbaths for continued dyeing.

Inonotus hispidus (Bulliard : Fries) Karsten Illus. p. 146

Fruiting body: 3⅛–6" (8–16 cm) wide, semicircular to fan-shaped, convex, stalkless, fibrous-tough when fresh; surface coarsely hairy, azonate, bright reddish orange when young, becoming dark reddish brown to blackish brown at maturity; margin blunt, curved.

Flesh: up to 1½" (4 cm) thick, fibrous when fresh, becoming brittle in age, azonate, dark reddish brown.

Pore surface: yellowish brown, becoming blackish in age, rough; pores angular, 1–3 per mm.

Spore print: brown.

Microscopic features: spores 8–11 x 6–8 µm, subglobose to ovoid, smooth, thick-walled, brown; setae absent to abundant, 20–25 x 6–8 µm, dark reddish brown.

Fruiting: usually solitary, on decaying hardwoods, especially oak and black walnut; year round; occasional; eastern and southern United States and the Pacific Coast.

Dye notes:

no mordant	◦	gold
alum	·	reddish brown
chrome	··	reddish brown
tin	···	brownish orange
copper	····	golden brown
iron	·····	brown

Inonotus obliquus (Persoon) Pilát Illus. p. 146

Fruiting body: a sterile conk, 4–15" (10–38.5 cm) wide, irregularly shaped, resembling charred wood or a canker-like growth, stalkless; outer portion black to dark brown or reddish brown, hard and brittle, deeply cracked; inner portion corky, bright yellow-brown to rusty brown.

Fruiting: solitary or in groups, usually on standing birch or sometimes on ironwood, elm, alder or beech; year-round, perennial; common; widely distributed across northern North America.

Comments: the entire conk is a sterile mass of fungal tissue. The actual fruiting body is seldom observed. It is closely attached to the wood and produces spores which measure 8–10 x 5–7 µm which are broadly elliptic, smooth and hyaline to pale yellow.

Dye notes:

no mordant	◦	beige
alum	·	light golden brown
chrome	··	light golden brown
tin	···	reddish brown
copper	····	light greenish brown
iron	·····	grayish brown

Inonotus rheades (Persoon) Bondarzew and Singer Illus. p. 146

Cap: 2–4⅜" (5–11 cm) wide, shape variable, fan-shaped, semicircular, circular and irregular, broadly convex, stalkless, moist, fibrous-tough and somewhat flexible when fresh, becoming dry and rigid in age, coated with a dense layer of fibrils which become matted in age; fibrils pale yellow-brown at first, becoming stained rusty brown from spores, darkening in age; margin incurved when young, often wavy at maturity.

Flesh: bright yellowish brown when young, becoming dark rusty brown, shiny; odor and taste not distinctive.

Pore surface: pale yellowish brown when young, becoming dark reddish brown in age; pores angular, often lacerated, 1–3 per mm.

Spore print: rusty brown.

Microscopic features: spores 5–6 x 3–4 μm, broadly elliptic, often flattened on one end, smooth, pale brown; setae absent.

Macrochemical tests: all parts stain blackish brown with KOH.

Fruiting: in groups or overlapping clusters on decaying trunks, logs and stumps of poplar; June–October; infrequent; distributed across the northern United States and Canada.

Comments: copious deposit of rusty brown spores is often observed on fallen leaves and plants beneath the fruiting bodies.

Dye notes:

no mordant	∘	beige
alum	·	golden brown
chrome	··	golden brown
tin	···	orange
copper	····	light brown
iron	·····	grayish brown

Inonotus tomentosus (Fries) Teng

Illus. p. 146

Cap: 1⅜–6½" (3.5–16.5 cm) wide, circular to fan-shaped or irregular, sometimes lobed or fused with adjacent specimens, fibrous-tough; surface dry, velvety or with matted hairs, coarsely wrinkled and uneven or smooth, tan to ochraceous or rusty brown; margin blunt, wavy to irregular at maturity.

Flesh: up to ¼" (6 mm) thick, fibrous-tough, yellowish brown to rusty brown; black in KOH.

Pore surface: buff at first, becoming grayish brown to dark brown in age; pores angular, 2–4 per mm.

Stalk: ¾–2" (2–5 cm) long, ¼–¾" (6–20 mm) thick, sometimes rudimentary, central to eccentric or lateral, nearly equal or irregular, velvety to felty, ochraceous to dark rusty brown.

Spore print: pale yellow to pale brown.

Microscopic features: spores 5–6 x 3–4 μm, elliptic, smooth, yellowish; setae present.

Fruiting: solitary, in groups or fused together on the ground, duff or decaying wood under conifers; August–February; fairly common; widely distributed across North America except the Midwest.

Dye notes:

no mordant	∘	light beige
alum	·	beige
chrome	··	beige
tin	···	orange
copper	····	light golden brown
iron	·····	light brown

Best color results are obtained using a 2:1 mushroom to wool ratio.

Ischnoderma resinosum (Fries) Karsten

Illus. p. 146

Cap: 3–10" (7.5–25.5 cm) wide, semicircular to fan-shaped, flattened to convex, stalkless, fleshy-soft when young and fresh, becoming fibrous-tough to brittle in age; surface concentrically and radially furrowed, faintly to distinctly zoned, velvety when young, later covered with a thin glossy resinous crust, dull brownish orange to dark brown; margin thick, rounded, whitish to ochre, exuding drops of water when fresh.

Flesh: up to ¾" (2 cm) thick, soft, becoming fibrous in age, whitish to pale yellow.

Pore surface: white bruising brown, becoming pale brown in age; pores angular to circular, 4–6 per mm.

Spore print: whitish.

Microscopic features: spores 4.5–7 x 1.5–2.5 µm, cylindric to sausage-shaped, smooth, hyaline.

Fruiting: solitary or in overlapping clusters on decaying wood; September–November; fairly common; widely distributed across North America.

Comments: Some authors consider *Ischnoderma resinosum* to be a species which grows only on hardwoods and recognize *Ischnoderma benzoinum* as a similar species which grows only on conifers. Other authors consider these two species to be synonymous.

Dye notes:

no mordant	∘	beige
alum	·	light brown
chrome	··	brown
tin	···	dark brown
copper	····	greenish brown
iron	·····	blackish brown

Best color results are obtained using a 2:1 mushroom to wool ratio.

Leptoporus mollis (Persoon : Fries) Pilát

Illus. p. 147

Cap: ½–1½" (1.2–4 cm) wide, rounded to semicircular or elongate, flat or slightly convex, stalkless, fibrous-tough; surface tomentose to glabrous, becoming wrinkled in age, azonate, pale pink or pale reddish purple at first, becoming purplish brown in age; margin colored like the disc or cream-colored, even.

Flesh: up to ¼" (7 mm) thick, soft to fibrous-tough, whitish to pinkish buff at first, becoming pale pinkish brown, typically azonate.

Pore surface: white to pale reddish purple when young, becoming brownish orange to dark purplish brown; pores circular to angular, 3–4 per mm.

Spore print: white.

Microscopic features: spores 5–6 x 1.5–2 µm, allantoid, smooth, hyaline.

Fruiting: solitary, in groups, or in fused clusters, sometimes resupinate or effused-reflexed on decaying conifer wood; year-round; occasional; widely distributed in North America.

Dye notes:

no mordant	∘	brownish pink
alum	·	pink
chrome	··	dark brownish pink
tin	···	brownish red
copper	····	light brown
iron	·····	reddish brown

Oligoporus caesius (Schrader) Gilbertson and Ryvarden

Illus. p. 147

Fruiting body: ¾–2⅜" (2–6 cm) wide, annual, sessile to effused-reflexed, rounded to fan- or shell-shaped; upper surface finely tomentose to strigose, whitish, usually with a blue tint, sometimes conspicuously blue, sometimes bruising blue; azonate; margin somewhat rounded.

Flesh: up to ⅜" (1 cm) thick, soft when fresh, white to bluish, azonate; odor not distinctive.

Pore surface: white to bluish; pores angular, 3–6 per mm.

Spore print: bluish.

Microscopic features: spores 5.5–7.5 x 1–2 μm, allantoid, smooth, hyaline.

Fruiting: solitary or in groups, sometimes overlapping, on decaying conifers or hardwoods; July–February; occasional; widely distributed in North America.

Dye notes:

no mordant	◦	none
alum	·	none
chrome	··	light grayish beige
tin	···	none
copper	····	golden brown
iron	·····	beige

A 2:1 mushroom to wool ratio was used for stated color results.

Oligoporus fragilis (Fries) Gilbertson and Ryvarden

Illus. p. 147

Fruiting body: ¾–2⅜" (2–6 cm) wide, annual, sessile or effused-reflexed, rounded to fan- or shell-shaped; upper surface tomentose to subglabrous, whitish to buff, staining reddish brown when handled or bruised, azonate; margin somewhat rounded.

Flesh: up to ⅝" (1.6 cm) thick, fibrous-tough, white then brownish as it dries, azonate; odor not distinctive.

Pore surface: whitish to buff at first, becoming reddish brown when bruised or on drying; pores circular to angular, 5–6 per mm.

Spore print: white.

Microscopic features: spores 4–5 x 1–1.5 μm, cylindric and usually curved, smooth, hyaline.

Fruiting: solitary or in groups on decaying conifer wood; June–November; occasional; widely distributed in North America.

Comments: *Amylocystis lapponica* is very similar but has much larger spores, amyloid cystidia, and usually has a strong iodine odor when fresh.

Dye notes:

no mordant	◦	none
alum	·	none
chrome	··	beige
tin	···	dark beige
copper	····	light greenish brown
iron	·····	dark beige

Phaeolus schweinitzii (Fries) Patouillard

Illus. p. 147

Fruiting body: a large overlapping cluster of flattened fused caps, or sometimes a solitary cap, attached to a solid central stalk.

Cap: 1½–10" (4–25.5 cm) wide, fan- to petal-shaped or circular, fibrous-tough; surface densely matted and wooly or hairy, faintly to distinctly zoned, dull orange to ochre when young, rusty brown to dark brown in age; margin yellow-orange to brownish orange, sharp, wavy, sometimes lobed.

Flesh: up to 1⅛" (3 cm) thick, fibrous-tough, yellowish to reddish brown.

Pore surface: yellow to greenish yellow or orange when young, bruising brown and becoming yellowish brown to dark rusty brown in age; pores angular, 0.5–3 per mm.

Stalk: ¾–2¾" (2–7 cm) long, up to 2" (5 cm) thick, branched or unbranched, enlarging upward, pale to dark brown.

Spore print: whitish.

Microscopic features: spores 5–9 x 3–5 µm, elliptic, smooth, hyaline.

Fruiting: solitary, overlapping clusters or rosettes on roots at the base of trees or on decaying wood, especially conifers; June–November, sometimes persisting year-round; fairly common; eastern Canada south to Florida, west to Colorado and California.

Comments: commonly called the Dye Polypore.

Dye notes:

no mordant	∘	beige
alum	·	gold
chrome	··	dark brownish orange
tin	···	orange
copper	····	brown
iron	·····	dark olive

An excellent dyer, proportions as low as 1:2, mushroom to wool, are all that is required to obtain fine colors. Do not change the pH when using *Phaeolus schweinitzii.*

Phellinus chrysoloma (Fries) Donk

Illus. p. 147

Fruiting body: ⅜–2" (1–5 cm) wide, flattened and semicircular to elongated, stalkless, fibrous-tough to woody; upper surface tomentose to hispid, sulcate, zonate, dull reddish brown to bright yellowish brown at the margin; margin typically wavy, slightly lobed, sharp.

Flesh: up to ⅛" (3 mm) thick, fibrous-tough, reddish brown with a thin black layer on the upper portion.

Pore surface: bright yellowish brown at first, becoming darker brown at maturity, glancing; pores angular to slightly daedaleoid, 2–5 per mm.

Spore print: brown.

Microscopic features: spores 4–5.5 x 4–5 µm, ovoid to subglobose, smooth, hyaline to pale yellowish brown; setae abundant, subulate, bright reddish brown in KOH.

Fruiting: resupinate at first, effused-reflexed to sessile in age, forming overlapping clusters or rows on decaying conifers, especially spruce; year-round and sometimes perennial; fairly common; northeastern and western North America.

Dye notes:

no mordant	∘	gold
alum	·	orange-brown

chrome	··	orange-brown
tin	···	brownish orange
copper	····	dark gold
iron	·····	dark brown

Phellinus everhartii (Ellis and Galloway) A. Ames

Illus. p. 147

Fruiting body: 2⅜–5⅛" (6–13 cm) wide, hoof- to fan-shaped, convex, stalkless, hard and woody; surface finely tomentose when young, becoming glabrous and crusty at maturity, typically sulcate and cracked, yellowish brown to blackish in age; margin thick and obtuse, bright orange on young specimens, becoming colored like the disc in age.

Flesh: up to 2" (5 cm) thick at the base, woody, granular, reddish brown.

Pore surface: dark yellowish brown to reddish brown and glancing with a golden luster when fresh, becoming dark brown in age; pores circular to angular, 5–6 per mm.

Spore print: brown.

Microscopic features: spores 4–5 x 3–4 μm, ovoid to subglobose, smooth, dark reddish brown: setae abundant, 15–35 x 5–10 μm, awl-shaped, thick-walled, dark brown in KOH.

Fruiting: solitary or in groups on decaying hardwoods, especially oak; year-round; fairly common; widely distributed in the United States and eastern Canada.

Dye notes:

no mordant	∘	light brown
alum	·	golden brown
chrome	··	orange-brown
tin	···	brownish orange
copper	····	light brown
iron	·····	dark brown

Phellinus gilvus (Schweinitz) Patouillard

Illus. p. 148

Fruiting body: 1⅛–4¾" (3–12 cm) wide, perennial, fan- to shell-shaped, somewhat flattened, stalkless to slightly effused-reflexed; upper surface slightly tomentose to glabrous, often wrinkled, zonate or azonate, dark yellowish brown to reddish brown; margin sharp.

Flesh: up to ¾" (2 cm) thick, fibrous-tough, bright yellowish brown, zonate.

Pore surface: dark purplish brown to dull yellowish brown; pores circular, 6–8 per mm.

Spore print: white.

Microscopic features: spores 4–5 x 3–3.5 μm, ellipsoid to ovoid, smooth, hyaline.

Fruiting: solitary, in groups or overlapping clusters on hardwoods, especially oak, sometimes on conifers; year-round; fairly common; widely distributed in North America.

Dye notes:

no mordant	∘	beige
alum	·	light golden brown
chrome	··	light golden brown
tin	···	orange
copper	····	greenish beige
iron	·····	grayish brown

Use 2:1 or 3:1 mushroom to wool ratio.

Phellinus robineae (Murrill) A. Ames

Illus. p. 148

Fruiting body: 3⅛–12" (8–30 cm) wide, perennial, shell-like to hoof-shaped, stalkless; upper surface azonate but marked by concentric ridges in age, finely tomentose, and yellowish brown when young, becoming deeply cracked to scaly and black at maturity, often developing large radial fissures in age; margin fairly thin and curved.

Flesh: up to 1" (2.5 cm) thick, azonate, woody, pale reddish brown.

Pore surface: dull yellowish at first, soon becoming reddish brown; tube layers pale reddish brown; pores circular, 7–8 per mm.

Spore print: reddish brown.

Microscopic features: spores 5–6 x 4.5–5 μm, ovoid to subglobose, often appearing flattened on one side, smooth, reddish brown.

Fruiting: solitary, in groups or overlapping clusters on black locust, rarely on other hardwoods; year-round; occasional to fairly common; widely distributed in the eastern United States, the Southwest, California, and Idaho.

Dye notes:

no mordant	◦	light yellow
alum	·	orange
chrome	··	orange
tin	···	brownish orange
copper	····	golden brown
iron	·····	brown

Best results were obtained using 2:1 mushroom to wool proportions.

Polyporus badius (Persoon) Schweinitz

Illus. p. 148

Cap: 1½–8" (4–20.5 cm) wide, circular to irregular, typically funnel-shaped or convex to slightly depressed, fibrous-tough; surface smooth, shiny or dull, pale reddish brown with a darker center when young, soon chestnut-brown to reddish brown with a blackish brown center; margin pale brownish yellow to pale reddish brown and incurved when young, becoming uplifted, thin, wavy or lobed in age.

Flesh: up to ⅝" (1.6 cm) thick, fibrous-tough, white.

Pore surface: white to pale buff; pores circular to angular, 5–7 per mm.

Stalk: ⅜–2" (1–2.5 cm) long, ⅛–⅝" (3–16 mm) thick, central or eccentric, nearly equal or tapering downward, smooth, reddish brown near the apex, black below.

Spore print: white.

Microscopic features: spores 6–10 x 3–5 μm, cylindric, smooth, hyaline; generative hyphae lacking clamp connections.

Fruiting: solitary, scattered or in groups on decaying hardwood; August–December; fairly common; widely distributed in North America.

Comments: also known as *Polyporus picipes*. *Polyporus varius* is smaller, up to 3⅛" (8 cm) wide, has a pale buff to tan cap with pinkish brown to grayish radial striations and a black stalk at maturity. *Polyporus elegans* is smaller, up to 2⅜" (6 cm) wide, has a nonstriate tan to chestnut-brown cap and a stalk which is colored like the cap on the upper portion and black below. *Polyporus melanopus* has a smaller cap, up to 4" (10 cm) wide, which is pale yellow-brown to gray-brown with radial fibrils, a velvety stalk, which is longitudinally wrinkled and black on the lower half or overall, and generative hyphae with clamp connections.

Dye notes:

no mordant	◦	light beige
alum	·	beige
chrome	··	beige
tin	···	light gold
copper	····	light olive
iron	·····	grayish beige

A 2:1 ratio of mushroom to wool was used to obtain results.

Polyporus melanopus Fries

Illus. p. 148

Fruiting body: mushroom-like with a cap and stalk; cap 2–4" (5–10 cm) wide, convex to broadly convex or sometimes slightly depressed, azonate, finely scurfy to appressed-fibrillose, dry to moist, reddish brown to grayish brown, or smoky blackish brown; margin sharp, often curved; stalk central, dark brownish black at the base or nearly overall, with a root-like underground portion.

Flesh: up to ¼" (6 mm) thick, firm, azonate, white, unchanging when exposed; odor and taste not distinctive.

Pore surface: decurrent, whitish; pores mostly angular, 6–8 per mm.

Spore print: white.

Microcscopic features: spores 7–9 x 3–3.5 μm, cylindric, smooth, hyaline.

Fruiting: solitary, scattered, or in groups on the ground, attached to buried wood of hardwoods or conifers; August–December; fairly common; widely distributed in North America.

Dye notes: *

no mordant	◦	beige
alum	·	light yellow-brown
chrome	··	beige
tin	···	light greenish brown
copper	····	brownish yellow
iron	·····	light greenish brown

Pycnoporellus fulgens (Fries) Donk

Illus. p. 148

Cap: 1½–3½" (4–9 cm) wide, fan-shaped to semicircular, flattened to slightly convex, stalkless, fibrous-tough; surface coated with tiny matted hairs, becoming nearly smooth in age, pale to dark orange to rusty.

Flesh: up to ¼" (6 mm) thick, corky to fibrous-tough, pale orange.

Pore surface: pale to dark orange; pores circular to angular, 2–3 per mm, often lacerated in age.

Spore print: whitish.

Microscopic features: spores 6–9 x 2.5–4 μm, smooth, hyaline, inamyloid.

Macrochemical tests: flesh stains red with the application of KOH.

Fruiting: solitary, scattered, in groups or sometimes overlapping clusters on decaying conifer or hardwood; year-round; occasional; widely distributed across the northern United States and Canada.

Dye notes:

no mordant	◦	pinkish beige
alum	·	light orange
chrome	··	light brownish pink
tin	···	pinkish orange
copper	····	light brown
iron	·····	beige

Pycnoporus cinnabarinus (Jacquin) Karsten

Illus. p. 148

Cap: 1⅛–5½" (3–14 cm) wide, up to ⅝" (1.6 cm) thick, fan- to kidney-shaped, flattened to convex, stalkless, fibrous-tough; surface wrinkled or smooth, orange to reddish orange, sometimes mixed with other colors in age; margin rounded or sharp.

Flesh: up to ⅝" (1.6 cm) thick, corky to fibrous-tough, reddish orange.

Pore surface: dark to pale orange-red; pores circular to angular, 2–4 per mm.

Spore print: whitish.

Microscopic features: spores 4.5–8 x 2.5–4 µm, cylindric to sausage-shaped, smooth, hyaline.

Macrochemical tests: flesh stains black with the application of KOH.

Fruiting: solitary, in groups, overlapping clusters or rosettes on decaying wood; year-round; fairly common; widely distributed across North America.

Comments: *Pycnoporus sanguineus* (Linnaeus) Murrill is very similar but it has thinner flesh (up to 3 mm), more intense and persistent orange-red pigmentation, and smaller spores that measure 5–6 x 2–2.5 µm.

Dye notes:

no mordant	◦	light golden brown
alum	·	light golden brown
chrome	··	light golden brown
tin	···	golden brown
copper	····	light brown
iron	·····	light golden brown

Pycnoporus sanguineus (Linnaeus) Murrill

Illus. p. 149

Fruiting body: 1⅛–3⅛" (3–8 cm) wide, semicircular to fan-shaped, broadly convex to nearly plane, thin, stalkless, fibrous-tough when fresh, becoming woody when dry; surface dry, finely tomentose near the margin, subglabrous toward the disc, azonate, orange-red, usually persisting or sometimes fading to salmon-buff in age; margin sharp.

Flesh: up to ⅛" (3 mm) thick, fibrous-tough, concentrically zoned with pale orange and pale buff in some specimens, azonate and orange-buff in others.

Pore surface: dark red; pores circular, 5–6 per mm.

Spore print: white.

Microscopic features: spores 5–6 x 2–2.5 µm, cylindric, slightly curved, smooth, hyaline.

Fruiting: solitary, in groups or overlapping clusters on decaying wood of broadleaf trees; year-round; occasional; New York south to Florida, west to Nebraska and Texas, also reported from Arizona.

Comments: *Pycnoporus cinnabarinus* (Jacquin) Karsten is very similar but it has thicker flesh (up to 1.5 cm), less intense and persistent orange-red pigmentation, and larger spores that measure 6–8 x 2.5–3 µm.

Dye notes:

no mordant	∘	light golden brown
alum	·	light golden brown
chrome	··	light golden brown
tin	···	light golden brown
copper	····	light brown
iron	·····	light golden brown

Trametes versicolor (Linnaeus : Fries) Pilát

Illus. p. 149

Cap: ¾–4" (2–10 cm) wide, fan- to kidney-shaped, flattened, sometimes laterally fused and forming extensive rows, stalkless, fibrous-tough, thin; surface velvety to silky, with conspicuous concentric zones; zones contrasting and variously colored, often with shades of brown, blue, gray, orange and green; margin thin, sharp, wavy, sometimes folded or lobed.

Flesh: up to ⅛" (3 mm) thick, fibrous-tough, white to creamy white.

Pore surface: white to grayish; pores angular to circular, 3–5 per mm.

Spore print: white.

Microscopic features: spores 5–6 x 1.5–2 µm, cylindric to sausage-shaped, smooth, hyaline.

Fruiting: solitary, in overlapping clusters, rows or rosettes; year-round; very common; widely distributed in North America.

Comments: *Stereum* species lack pores on their lower surfaces. *Trametes hirsuta* has a grayish to yellowish or brownish zoned cap, usually with a brown margin. *Trametes pubescens* has a finely hairy to smooth, creamy white to yellowish buff, azonate or faintly zoned cap.

Dye notes:

no mordant	∘	light gray
alum	·	blue
chrome	··	greenish blue
tin	···	dark blue
copper	····	light green
iron	·····	greenish blue

Trametes versicolor varies tremendously in color form. The above color results were obtained using the blue form in a 2:1 ratio of mushroom to wool. The non-blue varieties yield little to no color. See illus., p. 157.

Puffballs and Allies

Puffballs form fruiting bodies that are round, oval, pear- to turban-shaped, or irregularly rounded but *not* star-shaped at maturity. They are usually stalkless but are occasionally stalked. Puffballs grow on the ground or decaying wood, sometimes partially or completely buried.

Pisolithus tinctorius (Persoon) Coker and Couch Illus. p. 31

Fruiting body: 1⅜–4" (3.5–10 cm) wide, oval to pear-shaped or sometimes club-shaped in age, tapering downward to form a thick, stalk-like rooting base.

Spore case: a thin, smooth, shiny peridium, dingy yellow to yellow-brown, splitting irregularly at maturity to expose hundreds of tiny yellowish to brownish peridioles in a black gelatinous matrix.

Spore mass: reddish brown to dark brown and powdery at maturity, produced by the disintegrating peridioles.

Microscopic features: spores 7–12 µm, round, echinulate, brownish.

Fruiting: solitary, scattered, or in groups in sandy soil, typically under oak and pine, commonly with Prickly Pear cactus, often partially buried; July–December, sometimes persisting nearly year-round; fairly common to locally abundant; widely distributed across North America.

Comments: commonly called the Dye-maker's False Puffball.

Dye notes:

no mordant	∘	dark brown
alum	·	dark brown
chrome	··	dark brown
tin	···	golden brown
copper	····	dark brown
iron	·····	dark brown

Scleroderma meridionale Demoulin and Malençon Illus. p. 31

Fruiting body: ¾–2⅜" (2–6 cm) wide, globose to subglobose or irregular in outline, tapered downward to form a thick, stalk-like rooting base.

Spore case: moderately thick, up to 1⁄16" (2 mm) thick; surface dry, roughened, conspicuously areolate and warted at maturity, ochraceous-tan to bright ochraceous-yellow, with dull grayish to yellowish brown warts, slowly splitting into irregular lobes at maturity to expose the spore mass.

Stalk-like base: 1–3½" (2.5–9 cm) long, ¾–1¾" (2–4.5 cm) thick, tapered in either direction, with coarse irregular blunt projections, scurfy-roughened, dull ochraceous-orange to ochre-yellow or brownish, typically coated with sand.

Spore mass: dark gray to brownish gray or blackish gray and coarsely powdery at maturity.

Microscopic features: spores 12–20 µm, globose, echinulate, reticulate, dark brown.

Fruiting: solitary, scattered or in groups partially buried in sand; September–November; occasional; widely distributed across the northern United States and Canada.

Comments: Also known as *Scleroderma macrorhizon* Wallroth *sensu* Guzmán.

Dye notes:

no mordant	◦	pinkish brown
alum	·	brown
chrome	··	light brown
tin	···	light golden brown
copper	····	greenish brown
iron	·····	pinkish beige

Scleroderma polyrhizon (Gmelin) Lévielle Illus. p. 149

Fruiting body: 1½–4½" (4–12 cm) wide, round to oval or irregular when closed, expanding up to 6" (15.5 cm) and resembling a giant earthstar when open.

Spore case: wall ⅛–⅜" (3–10 mm) thick, hard, rind-like, rough, areolate to somewhat scaly, dingy white to straw-colored or pale yellow-brown, splitting open at maturity into 4–8 star-like rays and exposing the spore mass.

Spore mass: firm when young, becoming powdery, brown to purplish brown, becoming blackish brown at maturity.

Microscopic features: spores 5–10 μm, globose, coated with short spines, sometimes forming a partial reticulum, purple-brown.

Fruiting: solitary or in groups on or partially buried in sandy soil, often along roads or on hillsides; August–November; occasional; widely distributed in North America.

Comments: also known as *Scleroderma geaster.*

Dye notes:

no mordant	◦	light brown
alum	·	light golden brown
chrome	··	light gray-brown
tin	···	golden brown
copper	····	golden brown
iron	·····	brown

Tooth Fungi

Members of this group have downward pointing, spine-like teeth on which spores are produced. Although one species grows on fallen pine cones, most Tooth Fungi grow on the ground and form teeth on the underside of their caps. Other members grow on wood and have teeth along branches or at the tips of branches. One species, usually found on standing trees, resembles a satyr's beard and has long spines hanging from a stalkless, solid mass of tissue. They differ from similar tooth-like Polypores by forming conic teeth instead of elongated, flattened, irregular tubes. Much of the information in this section is based on the descriptions by Richard E. Baird (1986) and Kenneth A. Harrison (1968).

Always bring the pH up to 8 or 9 when dyeing with Tooth Fungi. This increased alkalinity produces better blue colors.

Bankera fuligineo-alba (Schmidt) Pouzar Illus. p. 149

Cap: 2¾–6" (7–15.5 cm) wide, convex to nearly plane, sometimes depressed; surface viscid when fresh, soon becoming dry, appressed-fibrillose, often pitted, whitish to pale brown or sometimes with a salmon tint, covered with a conspicuous layer of pine needles and other debris; margin often lobed or wavy in age.

Flesh: dull white to yellowish; odor and taste not distinctive.

Spines: subdecurrent, up to ⅜" (1 cm) long, white to yellowish.

Stalk: ¾–1¾" (2–4.5 cm) long, ⅜–¾" (1–2 cm) thick, nearly equal or enlarged upward, dry, solid, smooth, colored like the cap, with a white zone beneath the spines.

Microscopic features: spores 3.5–5 x 3–4 µm, subglobose, echinulate, hyaline.

Macrochemical tests: flesh stains pale olive or may be negative with the application of KOH or NH_4OH.

Fruiting: solitary, scattered, or in groups on the ground under conifers, especially pines; July–September; uncommon; eastern Canada south to Georgia.

Comments: *Bankera violascens* is very similar but has a slightly smaller cap, up to 5" (12.5 cm) wide, and lacks an adhering layer of pine needles on its cap.

Dye notes:

no mordant	◦	none
alum	·	none
chrome	··	none
tin	···	none
copper	····	light golden brown
iron	·····	beige

The reported color results were obtained using a 6:5 mushroom to wool ratio.

Bankera violascens (Albertini and Schweinitz) Pouzar Illus. p. 149

Cap: 1⅛–5" (3–12.5 cm) wide, convex at first, becoming plane to somewhat depressed at maturity; surface dry, finely tomentose to fibrillose, typically lacerate-scaly at least over the disc in age, pale pinkish brown to pale purplish brown or pale grayish brown, not readily bruising when handled; margin typically lobed or wavy in age.

Flesh: dull white to pale pinkish buff; odor fragrant like maple syrup when fresh, soon disappearing after being picked; taste not distinctive.

Spines: strongly decurrent, up to ¼" (6 mm) long, pale gray.

Stalk: 1⅛–2¾" (3–7 cm) long, ⅜–1" (1–2.5 cm) thick, nearly equal to tapered downward, smooth, sometimes lacerate-scaly, colored like the cap but usually darker brown, often whitish near the apex and dark brown at the base in age.

Microscopic features: spores 4.5–6 x 4–5 µm, subglobose, finely echinulate, hyaline.

Macrochemical tests: cap and flesh instantly stain dark olive-green with the application of KOH.

Fruiting: solitary, scattered or in groups on the ground under conifers or in mixed woods; August–October; rare; eastern Canada south to New England, west to Michigan.

Comments: formerly known as *Bankera carnosa. Bankera fuligineo-alba* is very similar but has a slightly larger cap, up to 6" (15.5 cm) wide, with a conspicuous layer of debris adhering to it, and it does not become scaly in age.

Dye notes:

no mordant	○	light beige
alum	·	light grayish beige
chrome	··	beige
tin	···	light grayish green
copper	····	light grayish green
iron	·····	light gray

The reported color results were obtained using a 6:5 mushroom to wool ratio.

Hydnellum aurantiacum (Batsch) Karsten

Illus. p. 27

Cap: 2–7" (5–18 cm) wide, convex, becoming broadly convex to nearly plane, sometimes depressed; surface dry, nearly uniform at first but soon breaking into irregular projections, cavities, and channels; uneven, tomentose, becoming matted in age, sometimes zonate, orange-buff to whitish at first, soon becoming orange-salmon then darkening to rusty brown or bay-brown with a rusty orange to whitish or sometimes tan margin.

Flesh: in cap buff; in stalk rusty orange; fibrous-tough, zonate; odor and taste pungent and disagreeable.

Spines: decurrent, 5–7 mm long, dark brown with grayish buff tips.

Stalk: ¾–2¾" (2–7 cm) long, 3⁄16–¾" (5–20 mm) thick, enlarged downward to a bulbous base, dry, solid, covered with a matted orange to brownish tomentum, with an orange basal mycelium.

Spore print: brown.

Microscopic features: spores 5–8 x 5–6 μm, subglobose, distinctly tuberculate, brownish.

Macrochemical tests: cap stains black with the application of KOH; flesh stains dingy olive with the application of KOH (Harrison, 1968).

Fruiting: solitary, scattered or in groups, commonly confluent and forming large rosettes, frequently concrescent, on the ground under conifers; July–May; occasional to fairly common; eastern Canada south to Florida, west to Colorado and the West Coast.

Dye notes:

no mordant	○	light gray
alum	·	dark greenish gray
chrome	··	dark greenish gray
tin	···	greenish gray
copper	····	grayish green
iron	·····	dark gray

Hydnellum caeruleum (Hornemann) Karsten

Illus. p. 27

Cap: 1 3⁄16–4 3⁄8" (3–11 cm) wide, convex to nearly plane; surface dry, soft and velvety on young growing portion, lacking zones; whitish overall, soon tinted blue, often entirely blue, gradually changing to brown or dark brown in the center.

Flesh: in cap zoned, blue to purple with brown; in stalk homogeneous or somewhat zoned, orange to orange-red sometimes with blue, especially in young fruiting bodies; thick and extremely fibrous-tough; odor not distinctive to slightly farinaceous or slightly of cooked meat; taste mild or slightly acidic.

Spines: decurrent, ⅛–⅜" (3–10 mm) long, crowded, whitish at first, becoming brown with pale tips at maturity.

Stalk: ¾–2⅜" (2–6 cm) long, 5⁄16–¾" (7–20 mm) thick, enlarging downward and typically bulbous or tapering downward, dry, solid; pale brown, becoming darker brown in age.

Spore print: brown.

Microscopic features: spores 4.5–6 x 3.5–5.5 μm, nearly round to oblong, coarsely tuberculate, pale brown.

Fruiting: scattered or in groups, often with fused caps, on the ground under conifers; August–January; frequent; eastern North America across Canada and the northern United States to the Rocky Mountains and western coastal conifer forests.

Dye notes:

no mordant	◦	grayish beige
alum	·	blue
chrome	··	greenish blue
tin	···	dark blue
copper	····	olive
iron	·····	grayish blue

Hydnellum peckii Banker

Illusts. pp. 149, 150

Cap: 1⅛–5½ (3–14 cm) wide, convex, becoming broadly convex to nearly plane and usually depressed on the disc at maturity; surface dry, cottony-fibrillose to somewhat velvety when young, becoming uneven with numerous rounded to jagged projections especially over the center, white at first, soon tinged pinkish, becoming dull brown to purplish black and shading to a dull pinkish margin in age, usually exuding drops of bright red juice when fresh and moist.

Flesh: fibrous-tough, faintly zonate, pinkish brown to dull reddish brown; odor fragrant or pungent, especially when dried, or sometimes not distinctive; taste acrid, even after drying.

Spines: decurrent, up to ¼" (6 mm) long, pinkish at first, becoming dull brown to blackish brown in age, often with paler tips.

Stalk: ¾–3⅛" (2–8 cm) long, ⅜–1⅛" (1–3 cm) thick, tapered downward or nearly equal, often with an enlarged base, sometimes radicating, dry, solid, somewhat velvety to roughened, colored like the cap or darker.

Spore print: brown.

Microscopic features: spores 4.5–5.5 x 3.5–4.5 μm, subglobose, distinctly tuberculate, grayish yellow to pale brown.

Fruiting: solitary, scattered or in groups on the ground under conifers; August–February; widely distributed in North America and especially common in the Pacific Northwest.

Comments: *Hydnellum diabolus* is a synonym.

Dye notes:

no mordant	◦	beige
alum	·	blue
chrome	··	greenish blue
tin	···	dark blue
copper	····	grayish green
iron	·····	greenish blue

Hydnellum pineticola Harrison

Illus. p. 150

Cap: 1⅛–5½" (3–14 cm) wide, convex, becoming broadly convex to nearly plane, sometimes irregularly depressed; surface dry, roughened, whitish pubescent at first, becoming matted and pale vinaceous-cinnamon to reddish brown or dull brown, occasionally with pink droplets in humid weather, staining vinaceous cinnamon then blackish brown when handled or bruised, margin whitish to vinaceous-fawn.

Flesh: in two layers, moist, zonate, dark cinnamon; upper layer thick and spongy; lower layer fibrous-tough; odor faintly fragrant to slightly acidic; taste slowly disagreeable.

Spines: decurrent, up to ⅜" (9 mm) long, pinkish cinnamon when young, becoming vinaceous-brown, paler toward the margin.

Stalk: ¾–3⅛" (2–8 cm) long, ⅜–1⅛" (1–3 cm) thick, enlarged downward to a bulbous base, dry, solid, felty, pale to dark cinnamon, base often radicating.

Spore print: brown.

Microscopic features: spores 4–6 x 4–5 μm, oblong to subglobose, angular, tuberculate, pale brown.

Macrochemical tests: cap and flesh instantly stain black with the application of KOH, and olive-black with $FeSO_4$; dried flesh flashes violet, then black and quickly fades to dull olivaceous with the application of KOH (Harrison, 1968).

Fruiting: scattered or in groups, sometimes confluent, often concrescent, on the ground under conifers, especially pine; July–November; fairly common; eastern Canada south to Pennsylvania, west to Minnesota, distribution limits yet to be established.

Dye notes:

no mordant	◦	light brown
alum	·	grayish green
chrome	··	bluish green
tin	···	dark gray
copper	····	olive
iron	·····	light greenish blue

Best results were obtained using a 6:5 mushroom to wool ratio.

Hydnellum regium Harrison

Illus. p. 150

Fruiting body: very complex, composed of numerous overlapping caps forming rosettes.

Cap: 3–7" (7.5–20 cm) wide, broadly convex to nearly plane, typically deeply depressed; surface dry, covered with matted hairs, sometimes eroded, spongy, violaceous-black, with concentric ridges and obscure zonations; margin rounded, radially striate, grayish white at first, becoming brownish gray to dark olive-brown in age.

Flesh: firm, brittle, color variable from pale brown to violaceous-black, zonate; odor variable from pungent aromatic to not distinctive; taste variable from disagreeable to slightly bitter, or not distinctive.

Spines: decurrent, very close, up to ¼" (6 mm) long, pale violet to dark purple when young, becoming grayish brown in age.

Stalk: 2–6" (5–15 cm) long, 1–3" (2.5–7.5 cm) thick, central, tapered downward to a narrow cord below, dry, solid, complex, giving rise to and continuous with the overlapping caps, pinkish cinnamon, sometimes with small cavities containing orange-yellow mycelium that are evident when the stalk is cut lengthwise.

Spore print: pale brown.

Microscopic features: spores 4.5–6 x 3.5–4.5 µm, oblong to subglobose, tuberculate, brownish.

Fruiting: solitary or in groups on duff under conifers; September–November; occasional; Pacific Northwest from British Columbia south to Oregon, Idaho, and Colorado.

Dye notes:

no mordant	∘	greenish gray
alum	·	black
chrome	··	black
tin	···	black
copper	····	greenish black
iron	·····	black

A good dye mushroom, try experimenting with lower proportions of mushroom to wool, such as 3:5.

Hydnellum scrobiculatum var. *zonatum* (Batsch) Harrison

Illus. p. 150

Cap: 1⅜–5½" (3.5–14 cm) wide, convex to nearly plane, often depressed to funnel-shaped; surface dry, roughened and irregular with pits, horn-like projections and ridges, with conspicuously concentric zones; marginal zone white with pinkish tints, staining purple-brown to brown-black when bruised; inner zones of various colors including dull pink, vinaceous-brown, dark rusty cinnamon and grayish black.

Flesh: thick, fibrous-tough, orange-brown to dark reddish brown; odor and taste farinaceous or not distinctive.

Spines: decurrent, up to ⅛" (3 mm) long, dark vinaceous-cinnamon with paler tips.

Stalk: ⅜–1⅜" (1–3.5 cm) long, ⅜–1½" (1–4 cm) thick, extremely variable because of fusing, typically enlarging downward; dry, solid, colored like the cap.

Spore print: brown.

Microscopic features: spores 4.5–5.5 x 4–4.5 µm, somewhat angular, coarsely tuberculate, pale brown.

Fruiting: scattered, in groups or fused together into masses on the ground under conifers and hardwoods; August–December; fairly common; widely distributed across North America.

Dye notes:

no mordant	∘	brown
alum	·	grayish brown
chrome	··	brown
tin	···	dark brown
copper	····	brown
iron	·····	brown

Hydnellum spongiosipes (Peck) Pouzar

Illus. p. 150

Cap: ¾–4" (2–10 cm) wide, convex, becoming broadly convex to irregularly plane, occasionally depressed; surface dry, uneven, azonate, finely tomentose, cinnamon-brown to reddish brown, sometimes with a grayish brown bloom, darkening when bruised, margin entire or sometimes with a concentric ridge of secondary growth, often misshapen because of fusing.

Flesh: in two layers; upper layer thick, spongy, dark brown; lower layer thin, fibrous-tough, cinnamon-brown; odor and taste not distinctive.

Spines: decurrent, up to ¼" (6 mm) long, dark to pale brown with slightly paler tips when young, darkening when bruised.

Stalk: 1⅛–4" (3–10 cm) long, ¼–¾" (5–20 mm) thick, enlarged downward to a very broad bulbous base, up to 2" (5 cm) wide, often fused and arising with several others from a thick, tomentose pad of mycelium, dark reddish brown to dull dark brown or grayish brown.

Spore print: cocoa-brown.

Microscopic features: spores 5.5–7 x 5–6 μm, subglobose, moderately to coarsely tuberculate, pale brown.

Macrochemical tests: sections of dried material in KOH produce a violet flash, then stain black, and a dark olivaceous-brown color leaches into the mounting medium (Harrison, 1968).

Fruiting: solitary, scattered, in groups, or fused clusters on the ground in hardwoods, especially with oak; July–November; fairly common; eastern Canada south to Virginia, west to Minnesota and Iowa, distribution limits yet to be determined.

Comments: *Hydnellum pineticola* (Harrison) is very similar but grows under conifers, especially pine.

Dye notes:

no mordant	◦	none
alum	•	light blue
chrome	••	light grayish blue
tin	•••	light gray
copper	••••	light olive
iron	•••••	light grayish blue

Hydnellum suaveolens (Scopoli) Karsten

Illus. p. 150

Cap: 1½–6" (4–15 cm) wide, convex, becoming broadly convex to nearly plane, margin with a broad sterile band, sometimes lobed or wavy; surface dry, tomentose, soft, irregular, uneven, dingy white at first, becoming dull brown at the center and gradually outward to the white margin.

Flesh: fibrous-tough, zoned with violet and brown; odor strongly fragrant; taste not distinctive, or somewhat spicy.

Spines: decurrent, up to ¼" (5 mm) long, pinkish brown to dull brown or vinaceous-brown.

Stalk: 1⅛–2" (3–5 cm) long, ⅜–1" (1–2.5 cm) thick, tapered downward, dry, solid, tomentose, bright violet, darkening when bruised; flesh zoned with dark blue and brown.

Spore print: vinaceous brown.

Microscopic features: spores 4.5–6.5 x 3–4 μm, oblong, angular, irregular and unevenly shaped, coarsely tuberculate.

Macrochemical tests: KOH stains the violet tomentum on the stalk blue-green.

Fruiting: solitary, scattered, or in groups on the ground under conifers; August–November; occasional; eastern Canada south to North Carolina, west to Michigan, and along the Rocky Mountains from New Mexico to British Columbia.

Dye notes:

no mordant	◦	light greenish blue
alum	·	greenish blue
chrome	··	greenish blue
tin	···	dark greenish blue
copper	····	greenish brown
iron	·····	greenish blue

Phellodon alboniger (Peck) Banker

Illus. p. 151

Cap: 1⅛–3½" (3–9 cm) wide, convex to broadly convex or nearly plane, sometimes depressed; surface dry, tomentose to smooth, grayish white with a gray center at first, soon becoming dull brownish; margin thick, blue-gray, becoming thin and paler at maturity, soft and retaining a fingerprint under pressure, darker when bruised.

Flesh: in the cap pale dull brown or colored like the cap surface; in the stalk firm and black; odor sweetly fragrant, stronger on drying; taste not distinctive to slightly acrid.

Spines: decurrent, up to ⅛" (4 mm) long, pale grayish.

Stalk: 1½–4" (4–10 cm) long, ⅜–¾" (1–2 cm) thick, tapered downward to a bulbous base, felted, pale to dark brown.

Spore print: white.

Microscopic features: spores 4.5–5.5 μm, globose to subglobose, coarsely echinulate, prominently apiculate, hyaline.

Macrochemical tests: dried flesh stains blue-green with the application of KOH (Harrison, 1968).

Fruiting: solitary, scattered, or in groups in sandy soil under conifers especially pine, hardwoods, or mixed woods; July–November; occasional; eastern Canada south to Virginia, west to Michigan.

Dye notes:

no mordant	◦	light bluish gray
alum	·	blue
chrome	··	greenish blue
tin	···	dark blue
copper	····	bluish green
iron	·····	dark greenish blue

A strong dyer, worth experimenting with lower proportions such as a 3:5 mushroom to wool ratio.

Phellodon atratus Harrison

Illus. p. 151

Cap: ¾–1½" (2–4 cm) wide, solitary or several fused, nearly plane or depressed; surface dry, smooth or with minute hairs over the center, zonate, purple to purple-gray with light bluish gray along the margin, staining blackish when handled or bruised; margin wavy or lobed, thin, sharp.

Flesh: double-layered in the cap with a thin spongy upper layer and a fibrous lower layer, blue-black; stalk also duplex, purplish to black; odor of sweet clover or burnt sugar both fresh and dried; taste not distinctive.

Spines: short decurrent, up to ⅛" (2 mm) long, tapering to a point, lavender to lavender-blue, bruising blackish brown.

Stalk: 1½–2" (4–5 cm) long, ⅛–¼" (3–7 mm) thick, tapered downward, dry, smooth or slightly roughened, purplish gray to black, bruising blackish brown.

Spore print: white.

Microscopic features: spores 3.3–4.5 x 3–4 µm, globose to subglobose, finely warted, pale brown.

Fruiting: scattered or in groups, often fused, on the ground under conifers, August–November; common; Pacific Northwest.

Dye notes:

Mordant		Color
no mordant	◦	gray
alum	·	dark blue
chrome	··	dark greenish blue
tin	···	dark blue
copper	····	dark green
iron	·····	dark blue

A strong dyer, good results might be obtained by using a lower proportion of mushroom to wool.

Phellodon confluens (Persoon) Pouzar

Illus. p. 151

Cap: 1½–3½" (4–9 cm) wide, convex at first, becoming broadly convex and typically depressed, very irregular and often concrescent; surface dry, conspicuously velvety, whitish to creamy buff to grayish or grayish buff when young, becoming dull brown to dark brown where the velvety layer wears away, margin even or lobed, usually with a narrow band of sterile tissue, white, becoming fuscous to dark brown when bruised.

Flesh: in two layers; upper layer soft, cottony, colored like the surface; lower layer zoned, firm, darker than the upper layer, staining dark brown when bruised; odor of rotting wood combined with fenugreek when dried (Harrison, 1968).

Spines: decurrent, up to ⅛" (3 mm) long, violaceous gray when young, becoming dark vinaceous-brown in age.

Stalk: ¾–1½" (2–4 cm) long, ⅜–1⅜" (1–3.5 cm) thick, usually enlarged downward, often fused, dry, solid, central or eccentric, very irregular, scurfy to felty, spongy at the base, colored like the cap.

Spore print: white.

Microscopic features: spores 4–5.5 x 4–5 µm, subglobose, echinulate, strongly apiculate, hyaline.

Macrochemical tests: flesh darkens with the application of KOH, and stains olivaceous with $FeSO_4$; dried material inert in KOH (Harrison, 1968).

Fruiting: solitary, scattered or in groups, usually concrescent on the ground in conifer or hardwoods; June–November; occasional; eastern Canada south to New England, west to Minnesota, distribution limits yet to be established.

Dye notes:

Mordant		Color
no mordant	◦	beige
alum	·	light brownish gray
chrome	··	light grayish brown
tin	···	olive
copper	····	bluish green
iron	·····	dark gray

Phellodon melaleucus (Fries) Karsten

Illus. p. 151

Cap: ¾–2¾" (2–7 cm) wide, nearly plane to slightly depressed; surface dry, finely tomentose, becoming appressed-tomentose, sometimes glabrous or shiny, typically wrinkled and roughened on the disc, often radially wrinkled, zonate, reddish gray to violet-brown becoming olive-brown to dark brown as specimens dry out.

Flesh: uniform, not duplex, somewhat brittle, reddish gray to grayish brown or reddish brown; odor slightly fragrant, especially on drying; taste not distinctive.

Spines: decurrent, up to 1⁄16" (2 mm) long, whitish to grayish at first, becoming reddish gray to grayish brown at maturity.

Stalk: ½–1¾" (1.2–4.5 cm) long, ⅛–¼" (2–7 mm) thick, nearly equal down to an enlarged and somewhat flattened base, tomentose to fibrillose, reddish brown to blackish brown.

Spore print: white.

Microscopic features: spores 3–5 x 3–4.5 μm, subglobose to globose, echinulated, hyaline.

Macrochemical tests: flesh stains dark olivaceous to blackish in KOH or NH_4OH.

Fruiting: solitary, scattered, or in groups, rarely concrescent, on the ground under oaks or in mixed woods with oak and pine; July–November; occasional; eastern North America from Canada south to Florida, and the Pacific northwest.

Dye notes:

no mordant	◦	light gray
alum	·	greenish gray
chrome	··	greenish gray
tin	···	dark greenish gray
copper	····	olive
iron	·····	dark bluish gray

Good results have been obtained using a proportion as small as 1:2, mushroom to wool.

Phellodon niger (Fries) Karsten

Illus. p. 151

Cap: 1⅛–2¾" (3–7 cm) wide, broadly convex to nearly plane, or depressed to funnel-shaped; surface dry, tomentose or rarely smooth, sometimes roughened and irregular with pits, horn-like projections and ridges over the disc, usually with dark colored zones present, whitish to grayish white or pale grayish at first, becoming smoky brown to olive-brown to blackish olive or dark purple toward the center, staining brownish black when bruised.

Flesh: in both the cap and stalk duplex; upper layer spongy, colored like the cap surface; lower layer hard, bluish black to black; odor fragrant and stronger when dry; taste not distinctive.

Spines: subdecurrent, up to ⅛" (4 mm) long, gray, staining blackish gray when bruised.

Stalk: ¾–2" (2–5 cm) long, 3⁄16–⅜" (4–10 mm) thick, nearly equal to tapered downward to a bulbous base and a mycelial pad, velvety to felted, blackish gray to dark purple.

Spore print: white.

Microscopic features: spores 3.5–5 x 3.5–5 μm, subglobose to globose, echinulate, hyaline.

Macrochemical tests: flesh stains blue-green with the application of KOH or NH_4OH.

Fruiting: solitary, scattered, or concrescent in sandy soil under conifers, especially pine or hemlock, hardwoods, especially oak, or mixed woods; July–November; occasional; eastern Canada south to North Carolina, west to Manitoba and Wyoming.

Dye notes:

no mordant	◦	light gray-blue
alum	·	gray-blue
chrome	··	gray
tin	···	dark gray-blue
copper	····	gray-green
iron	·····	dark gray

A good dye mushroom. Try experimenting with lower proportions of mushroom to wool weight, perhaps as low as 1:2.

Phellodon tomentosus (Fries) Banker

Illus. p. 151

Cap: ⅜–2⅜" (1–6 cm) wide, broadly convex to nearly plane but usually depressed to umbilicate at the center; surface dry, whitish when very young, radially fibrillose, becoming zoned with cinnamon-brown to yellow-brown and dark brown; margin often elevated and wavy, whitish to vinaceous-buff.

Flesh: up to 1⁄16" (1.5 mm) thick, pliant, leathery, pale brown; odor not distinctive or slightly fragrant of fenugreek, especially on drying; taste not distinctive or slightly sweet and biting.

Spines: decurrent, up to ⅛" (2 mm) long, white, shaded with buff in age, bruising vinaceous-buff.

Stalk: ¾–2" (2–5 cm) long, ⅛–¼" (2–6 mm) thick, tapered downward, often flattened and irregular, dry, solid, colored like the cap, arising from a felty layer of mycelium in the needle duff.

Spore print: white.

Microscopic features: spores 3–4 μm, globose to subglobose, finely echinulate, apiculate, hyaline.

Macrochemical tests: cap surface stains black with the application of KOH, and grayish then black with $FeSO_4$; flesh stains black with the application of KOH, and grayish with $FeSO_4$.

Fruiting: scattered or in groups or arcs under conifers; July–November; occasional to fairly common; throughout the northern United States and Canada.

Dye notes:

no mordant	◦	none
alum	·	none
chrome	··	none
tin	···	greenish brown
copper	····	golden brown
iron	·····	grayish beige

Without a pH change, the following results were obtained:

no mordant	◦	light golden brown
alum	·	light golden brown
chrome	··	light brown
tin	···	golden brown
copper	····	golden brown
iron	·····	light brown

Sarcodon fuligineo-violaceus (Kalchbrenner) Patouillard Illus. p. 152

Cap: 1–4¾" (2.5–12 cm) wide, convex to broadly convex or nearly plane with a depressed center, dry, smooth or with tiny flattened scales; pinkish brown to purplish brown or grayish purple, staining dark purple-brown to gray-brown when bruised or handled.

Flesh: thick, brittle, dingy pink to reddish or pinkish purple; odor fragrant; taste farinaceous to slowly acrid or disagreeable.

Spines: decurrent, very croweded, short, 1⁄32–⅛" (1–3 mm) long, pinkish brown to reddish brown with paler tips.

Stalk: 1⅛–3⅛" (3–8 cm) long, ⅜–¾" (1–2 cm) thick, tapering downward to a radicating base or swollen in the middle and tapering in both directions, colored like the cap or slightly paler, olive-black or blackish near the base, dry, smooth.

Spore print: brown.

Microscopic features: spores 5–7 x 4.5–5.5 μm, broadly elliptic, finely warted, pale brown.

Macrochemical tests: flesh instantly stains dark green then blackish with the application of KOH, and slowly stains bluish gray with $FeSO_4$.

Fruiting: solitary or scattered on the ground under conifers, especially balsam fir and spruce; July–October; infrequent; widely distributed in eastern North America.

Comments: also known as *Hydnum fuligineo-violaceum*.

Dye notes:

no mordant	◦	light blue
alum	·	blue
chrome	··	dark greenish blue
tin	···	dark blue
copper	····	light greenish blue
iron	·····	gray-blue

Sarcodon fuscoindicus (Harrison) Harrison Illus. p. 152

Cap: 1⅛–6½" (3–17 cm) wide, convex, becoming broadly convex to nearly plane and depressed; surface dry, nearly smooth at first, becoming roughened and scaly on the disc, appressed-fibrillose and wrinkled to finely scaly toward the margin, dark violet to violet-black, tinged reddish violet toward the margin.

Flesh: soft, brittle, dark slate-violet; odor and taste not distinctive or somewhat farinaceous.

Spines: decurrent, up to ⅜" (1 cm) long, dark violet to dull lavender with pale lilac tips, becoming reddish brown to pinkish brown in age.

Stalk: 1–4" (2.5–10 cm) long, ⅜–1⅛" (1–3 cm) thick, tapered downward to a narrow base, dry, solid, glabrous up to the apex, dark slate-violet.

Spore print: brown.

Microscopic features: spores 5–6.5 x 4.5–5 μm, broadly ellipsoid to subglobose, tuberculate, brownish.

Fruiting: solitary, scattered or in groups under conifers or hardwoods; September–January; occasional; Washington south to California, also reported from Colorado.

Dye notes:

no mordant	◦	light bluish gray
alum	·	blue
chrome	··	greenish blue
tin	···	dark blue
copper	····	greenish blue
iron	·····	dark blue

Sarcodon imbricatus (Linnaeus) Karsten Illus. p. 152

Cap: 2–8" (5–20.5 cm) wide, convex with a depressed center when young, becoming expanded and deeply depressed at maturity; surface dry, cracked and conspicuously scaly when immature and mature, pale brown becoming dark brown; scales brown to dark brown, erect, pointed, arranged more or less concentrically and less erect toward the margin; margin incurved and smooth when young, becoming plane and cracked or torn at maturity; undersurface covered with decurrent spines,

Flesh: white to pale brown, firm; odor not distinctive; taste mild or slightly bitter but not strongly bitter.

Spines: decurrent, ¼–⅜" (6–10 mm) long, pale brown tinted grayish when young, becoming reddish brown to dark brown in age.

Stalk: 1½–4" (4–10 cm) long, ⅝–1⅜" (1.5–3.5 cm) thick, enlarging downward; dry, typically hollow at maturity, smooth, pale brown when young, darkening in age.

Spore print: brown.

Microscopic features: spores 6–8 x 5–7.5 μm, subglobose, coarsely tuberculate, pale brown.

Fruiting: solitary, scattered or in groups on the ground in conifer or hardwoods; May–November; infrequent; widely distributed across North America.

Comments: also known as *Hydnum imbricatum.*

Dye notes:

no mordant	∘	light beige
alum	·	grayish green
chrome	··	greenish gray
tin	···	grayish greeen
copper	····	greenish beige
iron	·····	bluish gray

Sarcodon joeides (Passerini) Patouillard Illus. p. 152

Cap: 1⅛–4⅜" (3–11 cm) wide, convex, becoming broadly convex to nearly plane and depressed in age; surface dry, roughened and irregular, tomentose to finely fibrillose-scaly, pale pink-brown to ocher-brown, margin incurved at first, becoming uplifted and wavy in age.

Flesh: thick, brittle, pale pinkish lilac on exposure, soon darkening to dark violet; odor farinaceous; taste somewhat acrid to bitter and disagreeable.

Spines: decurrent, up to ¼" (5 mm) long, pale pinkish brown when young, becoming purplish brown to dull brown in age.

Stalk: 1⅛–2¾" (3–7 cm) long, ⅜–1" (1–2.5 cm) thick, nearly equal down to a pointed base, dry, solid, longitudinally fibrillose, often somewhat scurfy, purple-brown to pink-brown, blackish green at the base.

Spore print: brown.

Microscopic features: spores 5–6.5 x 4.5–5 μm, subglobose, coarsely tuberculate, brownish.

Macrochemical tests: cap stains olive then black with the application of KOH, and olive-green with NH_4OH or $FeSO_4$; flesh stains dark green with the application of KOH, brilliant bluish green with NH_4OH, and dark olive-gray to bluish gray with $FeSO_4$.

Fruiting: solitary, scattered or in groups, sometimes confluent, on the ground under hardwoods, especially oak; July–September; rare to occasional; eastern Canada south to New England and New York, distribution limits yet to be established.

Dye notes:

no mordant	◦	beige
alum	·	blue
chrome	··	greenish blue
tin	···	blue
copper	····	bluish green
iron	·····	blue

Sarcodon scabrosus (Fries) Karsten

Illus. p. 152

Cap: 1½–5½" (4–14 cm) wide, convex to nearly plane with a depressed disc, sometimes umbonate; surface dry, nearly smooth at first, soon breaking into conspicuous scales and furrows, pale chestnut-brown or pale pinkish brown when young, becoming dark reddish brown then blackish brown in age, margin usually lobed and wavy.

Flesh: whitish, sometimes developing pinkish or brownish tints after exposure, dull grayish to grayish green at the stalk base; odor farinaceous; taste strongly bitter or farinaceous-bitter.

Spines: decurrent, up to ⅜" (1 cm) long, pale grayish pink at first, becoming pale vinaceous-brown with whitish tips.

Stalk: 1–4½" (2.5–11.5 cm) long, ⅜–1⅜" (1–3.5 cm) thick, tapered downward or nearly equal to a narrowed base, longitudinally fibrillose, scurfy, dry, solid, pale pinkish brown to dark brown, blue-green to olive-black toward the base.

Spore print: brown.

Microscopic features: spores 7–9 x 5.5–7.5 μm, subglobose, coarsely tuberculate, brownish.

Macrochemical tests: cap stains black with the application of KOH; flesh stains blue-green with the application of KOH.

Fruiting: solitary, scattered or in groups on the ground in conifer woods; August–January; occasional to fairly common; widely distributed across North America.

Comments: *Sarcodon underwoodii* is very similar but its cap is pale brown and it grows on the ground in hardwoods.

Dye notes:

no mordant	◦	beige
alum	·	blue
chrome	··	greenish blue
tin	···	blue
copper	····	bluish green
iron	·····	light blue

Sarcodon subincarnatus (Harrison) Harrison

Illus. p. 152

Cap: 1½–5½" (4–14 cm) wide, broadly convex to nearly plane with a depressed disc; surface appressed-fibrillose when young, cracking into scales at maturity, vinaceous-buff to pale vinaceous-brown at first, becoming medium brown to vinaceous-brown then blackish brown from the disc outward in age, margin typically lobed and wavy.

Flesh: thick, firm, whitish with a vinaceous tint; odor farinaceous; taste farinaceous to bitter.

Spines: decurrent, up to ¼" (6 mm) long, whitish to buff at first, becoming pale vinaceous-fawn.
Stalk: 2–4¾" (5–12 cm) long, ⅜–2" (1–5 cm) thick, eccentric or central, tapered downward, dry, solid, fibrillose to scabrous, vinaceous-brown to dull brown, often developing blackish stains in age or when handled.
Spore print: brown.
Microscopic features: spores 5–6 x 4–5 μm, subglobose to globose, tuberculate, brownish.
Fruiting: solitary, scattered or in groups on the ground under oaks and pines; September–January; occasional; California, Oregon, and Washington.
Dye notes:

no mordant	◦	light bluish beige
alum	·	light blue
chrome	··	light bluish green
tin	···	light blue
copper	····	bluish green
iron	·····	light greenish blue

Sarcodon underwoodii Banker

Illus. p. 153

Cap: 2–5½" (5–14 cm) wide, convex to nearly plane, often somewhat depressed at the center at maturity; surface pale reddish brown, dry, cracked when young and soon developing small, flattened, more or less concentrically arranged, pale reddish brown scales that darken in age and become partially erect, especially over the center; margin incurved and smooth when young, becoming plane, cracked and wavy at maturity; typically free and extending up to 1⁄16" (2 mm) beyond the spines.
Flesh: in cap white; in stalk pale brown; firm; odor fragrant or farinaceous, sometimes not distinctive; taste instantly very bitter.
Spines: decurrent, 1⁄16–⅛" (1–3 mm) long, crowded, white when young, becoming brown with grayish tips at maturity.
Stalk: 1⅜–2¾" (3.5–7 cm) long, ⅜–½" (8–12 mm) thick, tapering downward, usually bent at the ground, with an abrupt, white, pointed base; brown to dark brown, dry.
Microscopic features: spores 6–7.5 x 5.5–6.5 μm, oval to nearly round, strongly warted, pale brown.
Fruiting: solitary, scattered or in groups on the ground in hardwoods; July–December; uncommon; eastern Canada south to North Carolina, west to the Rocky Mountains.
Dye notes:

no mordant	◦	light beige
alum	·	light blue
chrome	··	light blue
tin	···	blue
copper	····	bluish green
iron	·····	light blue

Boletus aereus p. 35

Boletus badius p. 36

Boletus carminiporus p. 37

Boletus edulis p. 37

Boletus hypocarycinus p. 28

Boletus illudens p. 38

Boletus mirabilis p. 40

Boletus projectellus p. 40

Boletus rubripes p. 41

Boletus spadiceus p. 42

Boletus speciosus var. *brunneus* p. 42

Boletus subvelutipes p. 43

Boletus zelleri p. 44

Chalciporus piperatus p. 44

Fuscoboletinus paluster p. 46

Gyrodon merulioides p. 46

Gyroporus cyanescens var. *violaceotinctus* p. 47

Phylloporus leucomycelinus p. 47

Phylloporus rhodoxanthus p. 48

Pulveroboletus ravenelii p. 49

Suillus americanus p. 49

Suillus cothurnatus p. 50

Suillus granulatus p. 51

Suillus grevillei p. 51

Tylopilus alboater p. 52

Tylopilus atronicotianus p. 53

Daldinia grandis p. 55

Polyozellus multiplex p. 56

Clavariadelphus ligula p. 57

Clavariadelphus occidentalis p. 57

Cystostereum murraii p. 59

Thelephora terrestris p. 63

Thelephora terrestris f. *concrescens* p. 64

Anthracophyllum lateritium p. 65

Chroogomphus rutilus p. 66

Chroogomphus vinicolor p. 66

Collybia acervata p. 67

Collybia iocephala p. 67

Coprinus atramentarius p. 68

Coprinus micaceus p. 68

Cortinarius armillatus p. 69

Cortinarius badius p. 70

Cortinarius bolaris p. 70

Cortinarius brunneus p. 71

Cortinarius californicus p. 71

Cortinarius cinnamomeus p. 72

Cortinarius corrugatus p. 72

Cortinarius croceofolius p. 73

Cortinarius croceus p. 73

Cortinarius limonius p. 74

Cortinarius marylandensis p. 75

Cortinarius phoeniceus var. *occidentalis* p. 75

Cortinarius sanguineus p. 76

Cortinarius scaurus p. 76

Cortinarius semisanguineus p. 77

Cortinarius tubarius var. *luteofolius* p. 77

Cortinarius tubarius var. *tubarius* p. 78

Cortinarius violaceus p. 79

Flammulina velutipes p. 79

Gomphidius glutinosus p. 80

Gomphidius subroseus p. 80

Gymnopilus liquiritiae p. 81

Gymnopilus luteofolius p. 81

Gymnopilus luteus p. 82

Gymnopilus penetrans p. 82

Gymnopilus sapineus p. 83

Gymnopilus ventricosus p. 83

Hebeloma mesophaeum p. 84

Hygrophorus conicus p. 85

Hypholoma aurantiacum p. 85

Hypholoma sublateritium p. 86

Inocybe angustispora p. 86

Leucocoprinus birnbaumii p. 87

Ophalotus olivascens p. 88

Paxillus atrotomentosus p. 88

Paxillus involutus p. 89

Paxillus panuoides p. 89

Pholiota albocrenulata p. 90

Pholiota aurivella p. 90

Pholiota flammans p. 91

Pholiota malicola var. *macropoda* p. 91

Pholiota squarrosoides p. 92

Pholiota velaglutinosa p. 93

Psathyrella velutina p. 93

Stropharia ambigua p. 94

Tricholoma vaccinum p. 95

Tricholomopsis rutilans p. 95

Amylocystis lapponica p. 97

Boletopsis subsquamosa p. 98

Daedalea quercina p. 98

Echinodontium tinctorium p. 99

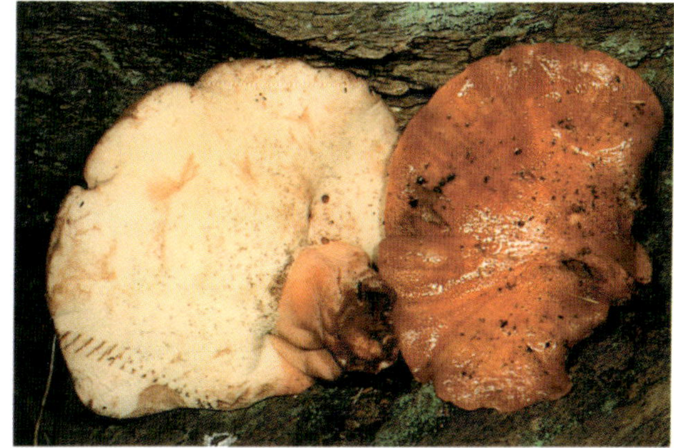

Fistulina hepatica p. 99

Fomes fasciatus p. 100

Ganoderma applanatum p. 101

Ganoderma curtisii p. 101

Ganoderma tsugae p. 102

Gloeophyllum sepiarium p. 102

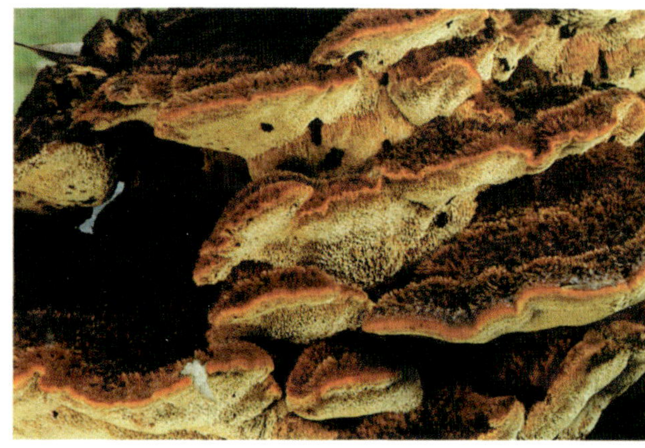

Inonotus hispidus p. 104

Inonotus obliquus p. 104

Inonotus rheades p. 104

Inonotus tomentosus p. 105

Ischnoderma resinosum p. 106

Leptoporus mollis p. 106

Oligoporus caesius p. 107

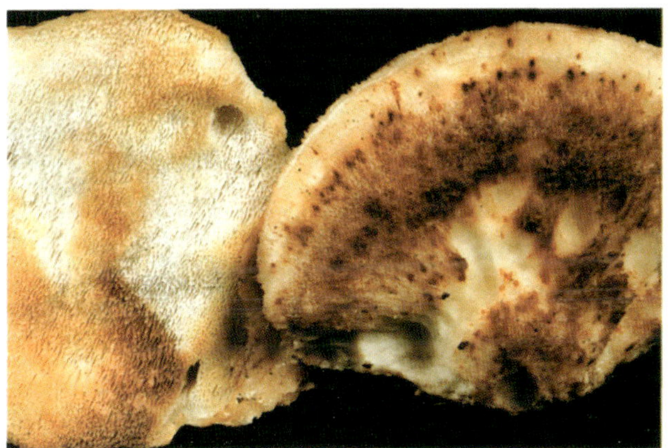

Oligoporus fragilis p. 107

Phaeolus schweinitzii (immature specimens) p. 108

Phellinus chrysoloma p. 108

Phellinus everhartii p. 109

Phellinus gilvus p. 109

Phellinus robineae p. 110

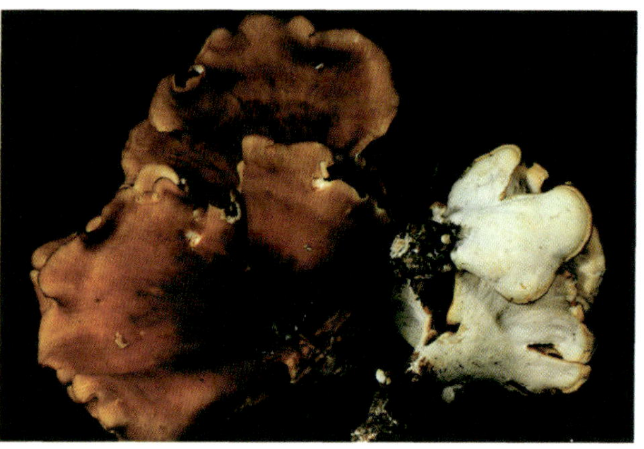

Polyporus badius p. 110

Polyporus melanopus p. 111

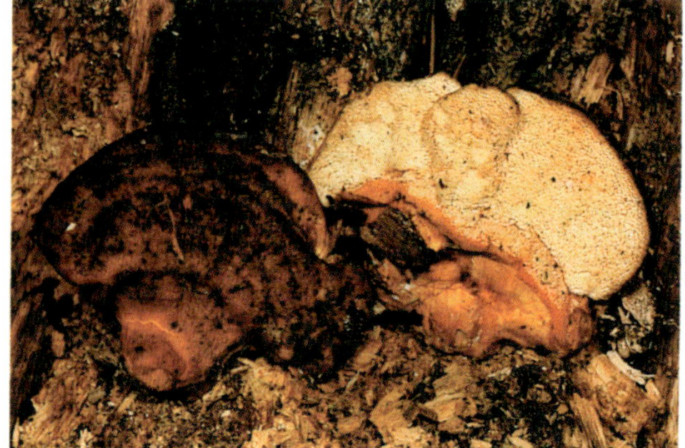

Pycnoporellus fulgens p. 111

Pycnoporus cinnabarinus p. 112

Pycnoporus sanguineus p. 112

Trametes versicolor p. 113

Scleroderma polyrhizon p. 115

Bankera fuligineo-alba p. 116

Bankera violascens p. 116

Hydnellum peckii (immature stage) p. 118

Hydnellum peckii (immature & mature stages) p. 118

Hydnellum pineticola p. 119

Hydnellum regium p. 119

Hydnellum scrobiculatum var. *zonatum* p. 120

Hydnellum spongiosipes p. 120

Hydnellum suaveolens p. 121

Phellodon alboniger p. 122

Phellodon atratus p. 122

Phellodon confluens p. 123

Phellodon melaleucus p. 124

Phellodon niger p. 124

Phellodon tomentosus p. 125

Sarcodon fuligineo-violaceus p. 126

Sarcodon fuscoindicus p. 126

Sarcodon imbricatus p. 127

Sarcodon joeides p. 127

Sarcodon scabrosus p. 128

Sarcodon subincarnatus p. 128

Sarcodon underwoodii p. 129

Examples of mushroom-dyed silk

Appendixes
Glossary
Bibliography
Index

APPENDIX A

A Note On Color

Color is so subjective. Perhaps one of the most difficult tasks in writing this book was reaching agreement on the difference between green-blue and blue-green, or deciding what was gold versus brownish yellow, or determining how light should light beige be before it was relegated to the "no color" or "none" category.

To simplify as much as possible, while remaining consistent and true to the color results we obtained as we saw them, we decided to use color ranges rather than common color names (e.g., purples, oranges, blues, rather than lavender, apricot, turquois). When a dye result is a blend of two different colors, we have used terms such as "blue-green," with green being dominant and blue being the modifier. The Mushroom Species Dye Color List is divided into the basic color categories: blues, browns, grays and blacks, greens, oranges, purples, reds, and yellows. Any mushroom that produces shades or varieties of these color groups is listed in the appropriate color section. All colors were interpreted using dried test strips viewed in sunlight against a white background. A piece of undyed, naturally processed, wool yarn was used as a negative color control.

Still, there will be disagreement with some of the color results as we have named them. There is bound to be variability due to the age of the specimens used, water type, fiber used, the varieties within any given mushroom species (see illustration of *Trametes versicolor*, below), and each individual's eye of perception.

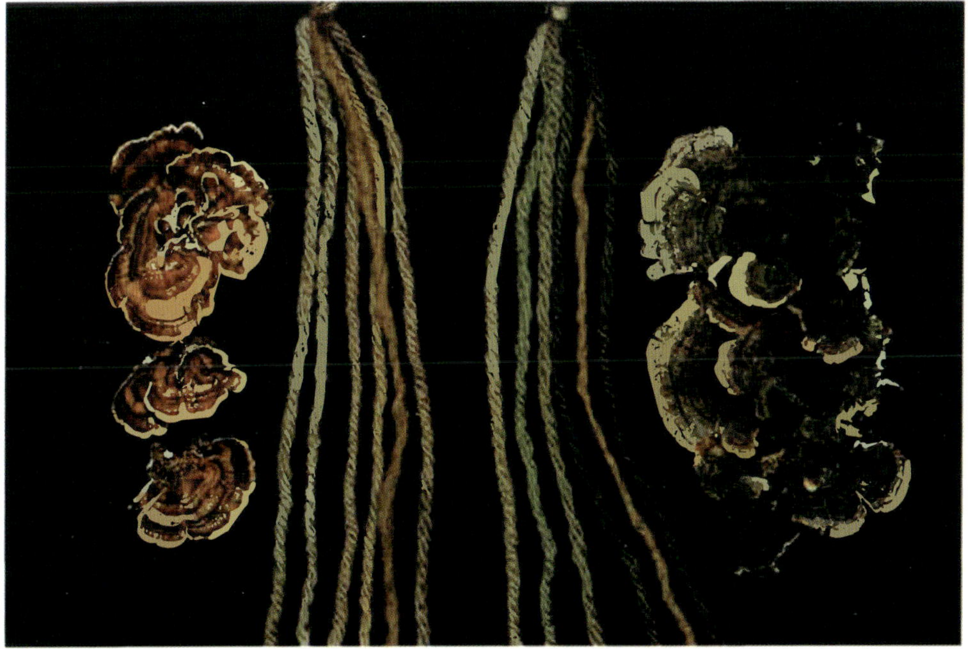

Example of varietal variations of *Trametes versicolor* and their dye test results (*left:* brown variety; *right:* blue-green variety)

Vest knitted with mushroom-dyed yarn

APPENDIX B

Mushroom Species Dye Color List

Blues

Collybia iocephala
Hydnellum caeruleum
Hydnellum peckii
Hydnellum pineticola
Hydnellum spongiosipes
Hydnellum suaveolens
Paxillus atrotomentosus
Phellodon alboniger
Phellodon atratus
Phellodon niger
Sarcodon fuligineo-violaceus
Sarcodon fuscoindicus
Sarcodon imbricatus
Sarcodon joeides
Sarcodon scabrosus
Sarcodon subincarnatus
Sarcodon underwoodii
Thelephora palmata
Thelephora terrestris f. *concrescens*
Thelephora vialis
Trametes versicolor (blue form)

Browns

Amylocystis lapponica
Apiosporina morbosa
Astraeus pteridis
Bankera fuligineo-alba
Bankera violascens
Boletus aereus
Boletus badius
Boletus carminiporus
Boletus hypocarycinus
Boletus illudens
Boletus miniato-olivaceus
Boletus mirabilis
Boletus projectellus
Boletus rubripes
Boletus spadiceus
Boletus speciosus var. *brunneus*
Boletus subvelutipes
Boletus zelleri
Chalciporus piperatus
Chalciporus rubinellus
Chroomgomphus rutilus
Chroogomphus vinicolor
Clavariadelphus ligula
Clavariadelphus occidentalis
Clavariadelphus pistillaris
Clavariadelphus truncatus
Collybia acervata
Coprinus atramentarius
Coprinus micaceus
Cortinarius armillatus
Cortinarius badius
Cortinarius bolaris
Cortinarius brunneus
Cortinarius cinnamomeus
Cortinarius corrugatus
Cortinarius croceus
Cortinarius limonius
Cortinarius sanguineus
Cortinarius scaurus
Cortinarius semisanguineus
Cortinarius tubarius var. *luteofolius*
Cortinarius tubarius var. *tubarius*
Cortinarius violaceus
Cystostereum murraii
Daedalea quercina
Daldinia concentrica
Daldinia grandis
Echinodontium tinctorium
Fistulina hepatica

Flammulina velutipes
Fomes fasciatus
Fomes fomentarius
Fuscoboletinus paluster
Ganoderma applanatum
Ganoderma curtisii
Ganoderma tsugae
Gloeophyllum sepiarium
Gomphidius glutinosus
Gomphidius subroseus
Gymnopilus liquiritiae
Gymnopilus luteofolius
Gymnopilus penetrans
Gymnopilus sapineus
Gymnopilus ventricosus
Gyrodon merulioides
Gyromitra esculenta
Gyromitra infula
Gyroporus cyanescens var. *violaceotinctus*
Hapalopilus nidulans
Hebeloma mesophaeum
Hydnellum caeruleum
Hydnellum peckii
Hydnellum pineticola
Hydnellum scrobiculatum var. *zonatum*
Hydnellum suaveolens
Hygrophorus conicus
Hypholoma aurantiacum
Hypomyces lactifluorum (+pH)
Inocybe angustispora
Inonotus hispidus
Inonotus obliquus
Inonotus rheades
Inonotus tomentosus
Ischnoderma resinosum
Leptoporus mollis
Leucocoprinus birnbaumii
Oliogoporus caesius
Oligoporus fragilis
Omphalotus olivascens
Paxillus atrotomentosus
Paxillus involutus
Paxillus panuoides
Phaeolus schweinitzii
Phellinus chrysoloma
Phellinus everhartii
Phellinus gilvus
Phellinus robineae
Phellodon confluens
Phellodon tomentosus
Phlebia incarnata
Pholiota albocrenulata
Pholiota aurivella
Pholiota flammans
Pholiota malicola var. *macropoda*
Pholiota squarrosa
Pholiota squarrosoides
Pholiota velaglutinosa
Phylloporus leucomycelinus
Phylloporus rhodoxanthus
Pisolithus tinctorius
Polyporus badius
Polyporus melanopus
Psathyrella velutina
Pycnoporellus fulgens
Pycnoporus cinnabarinus
Pycnoporus sanguineus
Ramaria abietina
Russula ventricosipes
Sarcodon imbricatus
Sarcodon joeides
Sarcodon scabrosus
Sarcodon subincarnatus
Sarcodon underwoodii
Sarcodontia setosa
Scleroderma citrinum
Scleroderma meridionale
Scleroderma polyrhizon
Stropharia ambigua
Suillus americanus
Suillus cothurnatus
Suillus ganulatus
Suillus grevillei (light & dark forms)
Thelephora palmata

Thelephora terrestris
Thelephora terrestris f. *concrescens*
Thelephora vialis
Tricholoma vaccinum
Tricholomopsis rutilans
Tylopilus alboater
Tylopilus atronicotianus

Grays and Blacks

Anthracophyllum lateritium
Apiosporina morbosa
Bankera violascens
Boletopsis subsquamosa
Clavariadelphus occidentalis
Collybia iocephala
Cortinarius bolaris
Cortinarius phoeniceus var. *occidentalis*
Cortinarius violaceus
Hapalopilus nidulans
Hydnellum aurantiacum
Hydnellum pineticola
Hydnellum regium
Hydnellum spongiosipes
Hygrophorus conicus
Leucocoprinus birnbaumii
Omphalotus olivascens
Paxillus panuoides
Phellodon alboniger
Phellodon atratus
Phellodon confluens
Phellodon melaleucus
Phellodon niger
Phlebia incarnata
Polyozellus multiplex
Polyporus badius
Ramaria abietina
Sarcodon fuscoindicus
Sarcodon imbricatus
Sarcodon underwoodii
Stropharia ambigua
Suillus grevillei (dark form)
Thelephora palmata
Thelephora terrestris
Thelephora vialis
Trametes versicolor (blue form)
Tricholomopsis rutilans

Greens

Bankera violascens
Boletopsis subsquamosa
Boletus aereus
Boletus mirabilis
Boletus speciosus var. *brunneus*
Clavariadelphus ligula
Clavariadelphus pistillaris
Collybia iocephala
Cortinarius cinnamomeus
Daldinia concentrica
Daldinia grandis
Fomes fomentarius
Gymnopilus luteofolius
Gymnopilus luteus
Hydnellum aurantiacum
Hydnellum caeruleum
Hydnellum peckii
Hydnellum pineticola
Hydnellum spongiosipes
Hygrophorus conicus
Hypholoma aurantiacum
Omphalotus olivascens
Paxillus atrotomentosus
Paxillus panuoides
Phaeolus schweinitzii
Phellodon alboniger
Phellodon atratus
Phellodon confluens
Phellodon melaleucus
Phellodon niger
Pholiota flammans
Polyozellus multiplex
Polyporus badius
Pulveroboletus ravenelii

Sarcodon fuscoindicus
Sarcodon imbricatus
Sarcodon joeides
Sarcodon scabrosus
Sarcodon subincarnatus
Sarcodon underwoodii
Thelephora palmata
Thelephora terrestris f. *concrescens*
Thelephora vialis
Trametes versicolor (blue form)

Oranges

Boletus aereus
Boletus badius
Boletus carminiporus
Boletus edulis
Boletus miniato-olivaceus
Boletus mirabilis
Boletus projectellus
Boletus zelleri
Chroogomphus rutilus
Cortinarius croceofolius
Cortinarius limonius
Cortinarius phoeniceus var. *occidentalis*
Cortinarius sanguineus
Cortinarius tubarius var. *luteofolius*
Cortinarius tubarius var. *tubarius*
Echinodontium tinctorium
Flammulina velutipes
Fuscoboletinus paluster
Gymnopilus liquiritiae
Gymnopilus luteofolius
Gymnopilus luteus
Gymnopilus penetrans
Gymnopilus sapineus
Gymnopilus ventricosus
Gyrodon merulioides
Gyromitra esculenta
Gyromitra infula
Gyroporus cyanescens var. *violaceotinctus*
Hypomyces lactifluorum
Inonotus hispidus
Inonotus rheades
Inonotus tomentosus
Phaeolus schweinitzii
Phellinus chrysoloma
Phellinus everhartii
Phellinus gilvus
Phellinus robineae
Pholiota flammans
Pholiota velaglutinosa
Pulveroboletus ravenelii
Pycnoporellus fulgens
Russula ventricosipes
Suillus cothurnatus
Suillus granulatus

Purples

Clavariadelphus ligula
Clavariadelphus occidentalis
Clavariadelphus pistillaris
Clavariadelphus truncatus
Collybia iocephala
Cortinarius californicus
Cortinarius marylandensis
Cortinarius phoeniceus var. *occidentalis*
Cortinarius semisanguineus
Echinodontium tinctorium
Gomphus clavatus
Hapalopilus nidulans
Hypomyces lactifluorum (+pH)
Omphalotus olivascens
Paxillus atrotomentosus

Reds

Chroogomphus vinicolor
Cortinarius californicus
Cortinarius marylandensis
Cortinarius phoeniceus var. *occidentalis*
Cortinarius sanguineus
Cortinarius semisanguineus

Cortinarius tubarius var. *luteofolius*
Cystoderma murraii
Echinodontium tinctorium
Hapalopilus nidulans
Hypomyces lactifluorum
Hypomyces lactifluorum (+pH)
Inocybe angustispora
Pycnoporellus fulgens

Yellows

Boletus aereus
Boletus badius
Boletus carminiporus
Boletus edulis
Boletus hypocarycinus
Boletus illudens
Boletus miniato-olivaceus
Boletus mirabilis
Boletus projectellus
Boletus spadiceus
Boletus speciosus var. *brunneus*
Boletus zelleri
Clavariadelphus pistillaris
Collybia acervata
Cortinarius corrugatus
Cortinarius croceus
Cortinarius limonius
Cortinarius scaurus
Fuscoboletinus paluster
Ganoderma applanatum
Gloeophyllum sepiarium
Gymnopilus liquiritiae
Gymnopilus luteofolius
Gymnopilus luteus
Gymnopilus penetrans
Gymnopilus sapineus
Gymnopilus ventricosus
Gyromitra infula
Gyroporus cyanescens var. *violaceotinctus*
Hebeloma mesophaeum
Hypholoma aurantiacum
Hypholoma sublateritium
Inonotus hispidus
Leptoporus mollis
Phaeolus schweinitzii
Phellinus chrysoloma
Phellinus robineae
Phlebia incarnata
Pholiota albocrenulata
Pholiota aurivella
Pholiota flammans
Pholiota malicola var. *macropoda*
Pholiota squarrosa
Pholiota squarrosoides
Pholiota velaglutinosa
Phylloporus leucomycelinus
Phylloporus rhodoxanthus
Polyporus badius
Polyporus melanopus
Pulveroboletus ravenelii
Suillus grevillei (light & dark forms)
Tricholoma vaccinum
Tricholomopsis rutilans

APPENDIX C

Dye Duds

The species listed below yielded little to no color when tested. Very light beiges, tans, and yellows were obtained from some, usually with tin or chrome as mordants. None seems to be dye-worthy.

Albatrellus caeruleoporus
Amanita muscaria var. *formosa*
Arctiporus fractipes
Armillaria mellea complex
Armillaria straminea
Bjerkandera adusta
Cantharellus cibarius
Cerrena unicolor
Chlorosplenium aeruginascens
Chroogomphus tomentosus
Coltricia perennis (East Coast)
Cortinarius camphoratus
Cortinarius claricolor
Cortinarius mucosus
Cortinarius pholidius
Cortinarius pyriodorus
Fomitopsis cajanderi
Galerina autumnalis
Ganoderma lucidum
Ganoderma oregonensis
Gomphus kauffmanii
Gyromitra korfii
Hebeloma velatum
Hericium americanum
Hygrophoropsis aurantiaca
Hygrophorus hypothejus
Hygrophorus speciosus
Irpex lacteus
Laccaria trullisata
Lactarius indigo
Lactarius paradoxus
Laetiporus sulphureus
Lentinus torulosus
Lentinus ursinus
Lycoperdon pyriforme
Macrolepiota rachodes
Morchella esculenta
Neobulgaria pura
Nigroporus vinosus
Octaviania ravenelii
Panellus serotinus
Phyllotopsis nidulans
Polyporus brumalis
Polyporus pubescens
Ramaria fennica
Ramaria sanguinea
Sarcoscypha austriaca
Scleroderma citrinum
Stropharia rugosoannulata
Suillus salmonicolor
Trametes cervina
Trichaptum biforme
Trametes versicolor (Non-blue varieties)
Tricholoma aestuans
Tricholomopsis decora
Tricholomopsis sulfureoides
Tubaria confragosa
Tyromyces chioneus
Xylaria polymorpha

Glossary

acidic: having a pH less than neutral
acrid: producing a burning sensation in the mouth
adjective dyeing: the process of dyeing using a mordant
adnate: attached to the stalk without a notch
adnexed: attached to the stalk and notched
afterbath: the dyebath remaining after the inital dyeing process
alkaline: basic, having a pH greater than neutral
allantoid: sausage-shaped
alum: aluminum potassium sulfate; a mordant
amyloid: staining grayish to blue-black in Melzer's reagent
anastomosing: fusing to form a network
annular zone: a poorly defined ring
apex (pl. **apices**)**:** the uppermost portion of the stalk, or the portion of the spore closest to the point of attachment to the basidium
apical pore: a small opening or thin area in the wall at the apex of a spore; also known as a germ pore
apiculate: having a short projection
apiculus: a short projection at or near the apex of a spore
appendiculate: hung with fragments of the partial veil
appressed: flattened onto the surface
appressed-fibrillose: having fibrils that are flattened onto the surface
appressed-tomentose: coated with a thick, flattened covering of hairs
areolate: marked out into small areas by cracks or crevices
aromatic: having an agreeable aroma
ascospore: a sexual spore formed within an ascus
ascus (pl. **asci**)**:** a sac-like cell in which ascospores are formed
attached: joined to the stalk
azonate: lacking zones
basal: located at the base
base: the lowest portion of the stalk
bloom: a dull, thin coating that is typically whitish
blooming: brightening a color, typically by adding a small amount of tin toward the end of the dyeing process
buff: pale creamy gray to creamy yellow
bulb: a swelling at the base of the stalk
bulbous: having a bulb-like base
button: immature stage of a mushroom
campanulate: bell-shaped
campanulate-convex: rounded and somewhat bell-shaped
cap: the upper part of a mushroom, which supports gills, tubes, spines, or a smooth surface on its underside
carbonaceous: black and brittle
central: attached to the middle of the cap
chrome: potassium dichromate; a mordant
chrysocystidia: cystidia that stain yellow or dark golden yellow in basic solutions such as KOH
clamp connections: small semicircular hollow tubes that join two adjacent cells by arching over the crosswall that separates them
clavate: club-shaped
colorfast: retaining color after repeated washings and/or exposure to sunlight
concave: depressed like a bowl
concentric: having rings or zones within one another
concrescent: growing together and fused
confluent: becoming continuous together
conic: shaped more or less like an inverted cone

convex: curved or rounded like the exterior of a circle
copper: copper sulfate; a mordant
corrugated: coarsely wrinkled or folded
cortinate: appearing spiderweb-like
cottony-fibrillose: composed of cottony fibrils
cottony-fibrous: composed of cottony fibers
cream of tartar: potassium bitartrate; a mordant used for brightening
crossveined: having tiny veins that connect adjoining gills
cuticle: the outermost tissue layer of the cap; also known as a pileipellis
cuticular: pertaining to the cuticle
cylindric: having equal diameter throughout the length
cystidia: sterile cells that project between, and usually beyond, the basidia
daedaloid: having tube mouths that are elongate and wavy
decurrent: descending or running down the stalk; a form of gill attachment
decurved: bent downward
deliquescing: dissolving into a black fluid
depressed: sunken
dextrinoid: staining orange to orange-brown or pinkish red to dark red or reddish brown in Melzer's reagent
disc: the central area of the surface of a mushroom cap
distant: spaced widely apart
duff: partially decayed organic matter on the forest floor
duplex: having two different layers
dyebath: the liquid extracted when mushrooms have been simmered and removed; the dyeing agent
eccentric: away from the center
echinulate: having small spines
effused-reflexed: spreading over the substrate and turning backward and outward at the margin
elevated: raised upward above the plane
ellipsoid: resembling an elongated oval with similarly curved ends
ellipsoid-oblong: resembling an elongated oval with somewhat flattened ends
elliptic: pertaining to an elongated oval with similarly curved ends
elliptical: pertaining to an elongated oval with similarly curved ends
elongate-suboblong: nearly oblong and elongated
emarginate: notched near the stalk
entire: even; not broken, serrated, or lacerated
equal: having the same thickness over the entire length
eroded: partially worn away and appearing ragged
evanescent: slightly developed and soon disappearing
even: stopping at the tube, gill, or spine layer, not projecting as a band of sterile tissue
expanded: enlarged and elongated
exuding: oozing out
farinaceous: having an odor of fresh meal or resembling cucumber
fenugreek: a plant with strongly sweet scented leaves
ferruginous: rust-colored
fertile surface: the spore-bearing surface
$FeSO_4$: iron sulfate, usually a 10% solution
fetid: having an offensive odor
fiber: a hair-like structure present on the cap or stalk of some mushrooms
fibril: a tiny fiber
fibrillose: composed of fibrils
fibrillose-scaly: with tiny scales composed of appressed fibrils
fibrillose-striate: having parallel lines or furrows composed of fibrils
fibrous: composed of fibers
fibrous-cottony: composed of cottony fibers
fimbriate: minutely fringed
flesh: the inner tissue of a fruiting body
floccose: tufted like cotton balls
floccose-fibrillose: tufted with fibrils
floccose-squamose: tufted with tiny scales
foetid: having an offensive odor
free: not attached to the stalk
fruiting body: the fleshy to hard reproductive structure of a fungus, commonly called a mushroom

fruiting period: a time during which a mushroom is likely to occur
fulvous: reddish cinnamon; colored like a red fox
fungus (pl. **fungi**)**:** any member of the kingdom fungi to include mushrooms, molds, yeast, and many others
furfuraceous: scurfy; covered with tiny particles
furrowed: having tiny grooves
fuscous: dark brownish gray to brownish black
fusiform: spindle-shaped and narrowing at both ends
fusiform-ellipsoid: elliptical but somewhat spindle-shaped
fusoid: somewhat spindle-shaped
fusoid-subventricose: slightly enlarged in the middle and somewhat spindle-shaped
fusoid-ventricose: enlarged in the middle and somewhat spindle-shaped
Gasteromycetes: puffballs and relatives which form spores in closed chambers within the fruiting body.
generative hyphae: one of three types of hyphae commonly found in polypores; typically thin-walled
genus (pl. **genera**)**:** taxonomic grouping of closely related species
germ pore: a thin portion of the spore wall through which the hypha passes during germination; also known as an apical pore
gills: thin to thick, knifeblade-like structures on the cap undersurface of some mushrooms
glabrous: bald; lacking hairs, scales, or warts
glancing: changing from dull to lustrous when the orientation of the pore surface is changed with regard to incoming light
glandular dots: sticky spots on the surface of the stem
Glauber's salt: sodium sulfate; a mordant that prevents streaking and ensures even distribution of color
globose: round
gluten: a sticky, glue-like, pectinous material
glutinous: having gluten
habit: the manner of growth, such as solitary, or in fused groups
habitat: the substrate from which the mushroom grows, such as among sphagnum mosses, on wood, or on the ground
hirsute: coated with hairs
hispid: covered with stiff, erect hairs
hemispheric: shaped like half of a sphere
homogeneous: composed of uniform cells or tissue
humus: decaying organic matter mostly of plant origin
hyaline: transparent; clear and nearly colorless
hygrophanous: appearing water-soaked when fresh, fading to a paler color as water is lost
hygroscopic: readily absorbing water
hymenial cystidia: cystidia that occur on the inner surface or edge of the tubes or gills
hypha (pl. **hyphae**)**:** thread-like filaments of fungal cells
inamyloid: unchanging or pale yellow in Melzer's reagent; neither amyloid nor dextrinoid
incurved: bent inward toward the stalk
inrolled: bent inward toward the stalk and upward
intervenose: having veins on the gill faces which often extend between the gills or from gill to gill
in the grease: wool fiber before it has been washed to remove the natural lanolin
iron: ferrous sulfate; a mordant
KOH: potassium hydroxide, usually made up in a 3–5% concentration in water; used to test color reactions
labyrinth: a maze contructed of intricate passageways
labyrinthine: having wavy lines that resemble a labyrinth
lacerated: appearing torn
lacerate-scaly: torn into scales
lacrymoid: shaped like a teardrop

lamellate: having gills
lanolin: the natural grease found in wool
lateral: attached to the margin of a cap
lobate: having lobes
lobe: rounded divisions of the margin
longitudinal: oriented along the vertical axis of the stalk; along the long axis of a spore or other structure
macroscopic: visible without the aid of a lens or microscope
margin: the edge of a mushroom cap
marzipan: a confection made with crushed almonds or almond paste
microscopic: visible only with a microscope
mordant: a chemical added to fiber that causes a certain color to bind to the fiber
mordanting: the process of adding a mordant
mycelium: a mass of hyphae, typically hidden in a substrate
mycorrhizal: having a mutually beneficial relationship with a tree or other plant
neutral: having a pH of 7
neutral dyebath: a dyebath at approximately neutral pH
NH_4OH: ammonium hydroxide; used to test color reactions on mushroom tissues
oblong: longer than wide, and with somewhat flattened ends
obtuse: rounded or blunt
ochraceous: pale, brownish orange-yellow
ochre: brownish orange-yellow
oval: shaped like an egg
ovoid: somewhat egg-shaped
paraphyses: sterile filaments located between asci
partial veil: a layer of fungal tissue that covers the gills or pores of some immature mushrooms
patches: see *warts*
perennial: continuing growth from year to year
peridiole: a tiny, egg-like structure that contains spores
peridium: the outer coat of a fruiting body; often divided into three separate layers
perithecium (pl. **perithecia**)**:** a minute, flask-shaped structure containing asci
pH: a measure of the acidity or basicity (alkalinity) of a substance
plane: flat
plicate: deeply grooved, sometimes pleated or folded
pores: the open ends of the tubes of a bolete or polypore
pore surface: the undersurface of the cap of a bolete or polypore, where the open ends of the tubes are visible
poroid: resembling pores or composed of pores
premordanting: the process of mordanting the wool before dyeing it
pruinose: appearing finely powdered
pubescent: having short, soft, downy hairs
pulverulent: powdery
pulvinate: shaped like a cushion, slightly convex
punctate: marked with tiny points, dots, scales, or spots
pungent: sharp or irritating
radial: pointed away from a common central point, like the spokes of a wheel
radicating: forming a root-like extension in the ground
ray: the split and pointed outer portion of the peridium
resupinate: spreading out on the substrate and not forming any projections
reticulate: covered with a net-like pattern of ridges
reticulation: raised, net-like ridges
reticulum: a system of raised, net-like ridges found on the stalk surface or spores of some mushrooms
rhizomorph: a group of thick, rope-like strands of hyphae growing together as a single organized unit
rimose: having distinct cracks or crevices
rimose-areolate: cracked and forming tiny patches

ring: remnants of a partial veil that remains attached to the stalk after the veil ruptures
rosette: a circular cluster with the shape of rose petals
rudimentary: basic; elementary; inconspicuous
rugose: wrinkled
saddening: darkening colors, usually with the addition of iron toward the end of the dyeing process
scabrous: having short, rigid projections
scale: an erect, flattened, or recurved projection or torn portion of the cap or stalk surface
scouring: washing and heating wool in order to release excess grease and debris
scurfy: roughened by tiny flakes or scales
seceding: attached at first and later separating
semicircular: half of a circle
septum: a crosswall
sessile: lacking a stalk
setae: sharply pointed sterile cells that are usually brown or yellow and project on the surface of the stalk or other portion of the fruiting body of some mushrooms
simultaneous mordanting: the process of using a mordant while the wool is being dyed
sinuate: gradually narrowed and becoming concave near the stalk
skein: a loosely coiled length of yarn
spines: tapered, typically downward-pointing projections on some mushroom cap's undersurface
spore: a microscopic reproductive cell with the ability to germinate and form hyphae
spore case: a structure containing the spore mass in species of Gasteromycetes
spore mass: a dense layer of spores
spore print: a deposit of spores, on a piece of paper or glass, from a mushroom's gills, tubes, or other spore-producing structures
stalk: the structure that arises from the substrate and supports the cap or spore case of a mushroom
sterile surface: a portion that lacks reproductive structures
sterile tissue: tissue not directly involved with the reproductive process
striate: having small, more or less parallel lines or furrows
strigose: covered with long hairs
subcircular: nearly round
subcylindric: nearly cylindric
subdecurrent: extending slightly down the stalk
subdepressed: slightly depressed
subdistant: gill spacing halfway between close and distant
subellipsoid: somewhat ellipsoid
subelliptic: somewhat elliptic
subelliptical: somewhat elliptic
subfusiform: nearly spindle-shaped
subfusoid: somewhat spindle-shaped; tapered slightly at both ends
subfusoid-ellipsoid: somewhat spindle-shaped and somewhat elliptic
subglabrous: nearly bald
subglobose: nearly round
submembranous: somewhat membranous
subovoid: nearly ovoid
substantive dyeing: the process of dyeing without the addition of a mordant
substrate: organic matter that serves as a food source for a fungal mycelium
subtomentose: somewhat covered with matted hairs
subulate: awl-shaped
subumbonate: having a slight umbo
subvelutinous: somewhat velvety
subventricose: slightly swollen in the middle and tapered to somewhat of a point
subviscid: slightly sticky or tacky
sulcate: grooved; deeper than striate, less than plicate
superior: located on the upper portion
tawny: dull yellowish brown
teeth: spines that point downward
terete: rounded like a broom handle

tin: stannous chloride; a mordant
tomentose: coated with a thick, matted covering of hairs
tomentum: coated with soft fibrils
translucent-striate: appearing striate when gill edges are viewed through moist, nearly transparent cap tissue
trilobate: having three lobes
truncate: appearing cut off at the end
tuberculate: roughened by small warts or bumps
tuberculate-striate: having striations that are roughened by small warts or bumps
tube layer: the portion of a fruiting body made up of tubes
tubes: narrow, parallel, spore-producing cylinders on the undersurface of the cap of a bolete or polypore
umbilicate: having a central depression
umbo: a pointed or rounded elevation at the center of a mushroom cap
umbonate: having an umbo
universal veil: a layer of fungal tissue that completely encloses immature stages of some mushrooms
uplifted: elevated toward the plane
utriform: bottle-shaped
veil: a layer of fungal tissue that covers all or part of some immature mushrooms (see *universal veil* and *partial veil*)
velvety-subtomentose: covered with velvety, somewhat matted hairs
velvety-tomentose: covered with velvety, matted hairs
ventricose: swollen in the middle and tapering to somewhat of a point
verrucose: warted
verruculose: minutely warted
vesiculose: having tiny sacs or bladder-like vesicles
vinaceous: pinkish red to pale purplish red
viscid: sticky or tacky
volva: a typically cup-like sac that remains around the base of a mushroom stalk when the universal veil ruptures
warted: having warts
warts: small patches of tissue that remain on the top of a mushroom cap when the universal veil ruptures
zonations: concentric bands of different colors on the surface of the cap or stalk of some mushrooms
zoned: having zones
zones: concentric bands of different colors on the surface of the cap or stalk of some mushrooms

Bibliography

Baird, R. E. 1987. Study of the stipitate hydnums from the Southern Applachian Mountains—Genera: *Bankera, Hydnellum, Phellodon, Sarcodon. Bibliotheca Mycologica.* Band 104: 1–156.

Bessette, A. E. 1988. *Mushrooms of the Adirondacks: A Field Guide.* North Country Books, Utica, New York. 145 pp.

Bessette, A. E., A. R. Bessette, and D. W. Fischer. 1997. *Mushrooms of Northeastern North America.* Syracuse Univ. Press, Syracuse, N.Y. 584 pp.

Bessette, A. E., O. K. Miller, A. R. Bessette, and H. H. Miller. 1995. *Mushrooms of North America in Color: A Field Guide Companion to Seldom-Illustrated Fungi.* Syracuse Univ. Press, Syracuse, N.Y. 188 pp.

Bessette, A. E., W. C. Roody, and A. R. Bessette. 2000. *North American Boletes: A Guide to the Fleshy Pored Mushrooms.* Syracuse Univ. Press, Syracuse, N.Y. 400 pp.

Bessette, A. E., and W. J. Sundberg. 1987. *Mushrooms: A Quick Reference Guide to Mushrooms of North America.* Macmillan, New York. 174 pp.

Casselman, K. L. 1993. *Craft of the Dyer-Colour from Plants and Lichens.* Dover, New York. 249 pp.

Gilbertson, R. L., and L. Ryvarden. 1986. *North American Polypores Vol. 1.* Fungiflora, Oslo. 433 pp.

———. 1987. *North American Polypores. Vol. 2.* Fungiflora, Oslo. 451 pp.

Harrison, K. A. 1968. Studies on the Hydnums of Michigan. I. Genera *Phellodon, Bankera, Hydnellum. The Michigan Botanist.* 7: 212–64.

Lundmark, H. K., and H. Marklund. 1989. *Färga Garn Med Svamp.* Brevskolan, Stockholm. 32 pp.

Phillips, R. 1991. *Mushrooms of North America.* Little, Brown and Company, Boston. 319 pp.

Rice, M. C. 1980. *Mushrooms for Color.* Mad River Press, Inc., Eureka, California. 154 pp.

Display at the 8th International Fungi & Fibre Symposium

Index

Albatrellus caeruleoporus, 164
Amanita muscaria var. *formosa,* 164
Amylocystis lapponica, 97, *144*
Anthracophyllum lateritium, 65, *135*
Apiosporina morbosa, 54
Arctiporus fractipes, 164
Armillaria mellea complex, 164
Armillaria straminea, 164
Astraeus pteridis, *30,* 61
Bankera
  carnosa, 116
  fuligineo-alba, 116, *149*
  violascens, 116, *149*
Bjerkandera adusta, 164
Boletopsis subsquamosa, 98, *144*
Boletellus projectellus, 41
Boletinellus meruliodes, 46
Boletus
  aereus, 35
  badius, 36
  carminiporus, 37
  edulis, 37
  hypocarycinus, 38
  illudens, 38
  luridiformis, 38
  miniato-olivaceus, 39
  mirabilis, 40
  piperatus, 45
  projectellus, 40
  rubripes, 41
  sensibilis, 40
  spadiceus, 42
  speciosus var. *brunneus,* 42
  subvelutipes, 43
  tenax, 39
  zelleri, 44
Cantharellus cibarius, 164
Cerrena unicolor, 98, 164
Chalciporus
  piperatus, 44
  rubinellus, 45
Chlorosplenium aeruginascens, 164
Chroogomphus
  jamaicensis, 67
  rutilus, 66, *135*
  tomentosus, 164
  vinicolor, 66, *135*
Clavariadelphus
  ligula, 57, *134*
  occidentalis, 57, *134*
  pistillaris, *29,* 58
  truncatus, *29,* 58
Collybia
  acervata, 67, *136*
  iocephala, 67, *136*
Coltricia perennis, 164
Coprinus
  atramentarius, 68, *136*
  micaceus, 68, *136*
Cortinarius
  armillatus, 69, *136*
  badius, 70, *136*
  bolaris, 70, *137*
  brunneus, 71, *137*
  californicus, 71, *137*
  camphoratus, 164
  cinnamomeus, 72, *137*
  claricolor, 164
  corrugatus, 72, *137*
  croceofolius, 73, *137*
  croceus, 73, *138*
  herpeticus, 77
  limonius, 74, *138*
  malicorius, 73
  marylandensis, 75, *138*
  mucosus, 164
  phoeniceus var. *occidentalis,* 75, *138*
  pholidius, 164
  pyridorus, 164
  sanguineus, 76, *138*
  scaurus, 76, *138*
  semisanguineus, 77, *139*

tubarius var. *luteofolius*, 77, *139*
tubarius var. *tubarius*, 78, *139*
violaceus, 79, *139*
whitei, 74
Cystostereum murraii, 59, *135*
Daedalea quercina, 98, *144*
Daedaleopsis confragosa, 98
Daldinia
concentrica, 54
grandis, 55
Dibotryon morbosum, 54
Echinodontium tinctorium, 99, *145*
Fistulina hepatica, 99, *145*
Flammulina velutipes, 79, *139*
Fomes
fasciatus, 100, *145*
fomentarius, *28*, 100
Fomitopsis cajanderi, 164
Fuscoboletinus paluster, 146
Galerina autumnalis, 164
Ganoderma
applanatum, 101, *145*
curtisii, 101, *145*
lucidum, 101, *164*
oregonensis, 164
tsugae, 102, *145*
Gleophyllum
sepiarium, 102, *146*
trabeum, 103
Gomphidius
glutinosus, 80, *139*
subroseus, 80, *140*
Gomphus
clavatus, 55
kauffmanii, 164
Gymnopilus
liquiritiae, 81, *140*
luteofolius, 81, *140*
luteus, 82, *140*
penetrans, 82, *140*
sapineus, 83, *140*
spectabilis, 82
ventricosus, 83, *141*
Gymnopus
acervatus, 67
iocephalus, 68
Gyrodon merulioides, 46
Gyromitra
esculenta, *28*, 62
infula, *28*, 62
korfii, 164
Gyroporus cyanescens var. *violaceotinctus*, 47, *132*
Gyroporus cyanescens var. *cyanescens*, 47
Hapalopilus nidulans, *28*, 103
Hebeloma
mesophaeum, 84, *141*
velatum, 164
Hericium americanum, 164
Hydnellum
aurantiacum, *27*, 117
caeruleum, *27*, 117
diabolus, 118
peckii, 118, *149*, *150*
pineticola, 119, *150*
regium, 119, *150*
scrobiculatum var. *zonatum*, 120, *150*
spongiosipes, 120, *150*
suaveolens, 121, *151*
Hydnum
fuligineo-violaceum, 126
imbricatum, 127
Hygnocybe conica, 85
Hygrophoropsis aurantiaca, 164
Hygrophorus
conicus, 85, *141*
hypothejus, 164
speciosus, 164
Hypholoma
aurantiaca, 85, *141*
sublateritium, 86, *141*
Hypomyces lactifluorum, *31*, 96
Inocybe angustispora, 86, *141*
Inonotus
hispidus, 104, *146*
obliquus, 104, *146*
rheades, 104, *146*
tomentosus, 105, *146*
Irpex lacteus, 164
Ischnoderma
benzoinum, 106
resinosum, 106, *146*
Laccaria trullisata, 164
Lacrymaria velutina, 94

Lactarius
indigo, 164
paradoxus, 164
Laetiporus sulphureus, 164
Lentinus
betulina, 103
torulosus, 164
ursinus, 164
Leptoporus mollis, 106, *147*
Leucocoprinus birnbaumii, 87, *142*
Lycoperdon pyriforme, 164
Macrolepiota rachodes, 164
Merulius
incarnatus, 60
tremellosus, 60
Morchella esculenta, 164
Naematoloma
aurantiacum, *85*
sublateritium, *86*
Neobulgaria pura, 164
Nigroporus vinosus, 164
Octaviania ravenelii, 164
Oligoporus
caesius, 107, *147*
fragilis, 107, *147*
Omphalotus olivascens, 88, *142*
Panellus serotinus, 164
Paxillus
atrotomentosus, 88, *142*
involutus, 89, *142*
panuoides, 89, *142*
Phaeolus schweinitzii, 108, *147*
Phellinus
chrysoloma, 108, *147*
everhartii, 109, *147*
gilvus, 109, *148*
robineae, 110, *148*
Phellodon
alboniger, 122, *151*
atratus, 122, *151*
confluens, 123, *151*
melaleucus, 124, *151*
niger, 124, *151*
tomentosus, 125, *151*
Phlebia
incarnata, *31*, 60
tremellosa, 60
Pholiota
albocrenulata, 90, *142*
aurivella, 90, *143*
flammans, 91, *143*
malicola var. *macropoda*, 91, *143*
squarrosa, *27*, 92
squarrosoides, 92, *143*
velaglutinosa, 93, *143*
Phylloporus
leucomycelinus, 47
rhodoxanthus, 48
rhodoxanthus ssp. *albomycelinus*, 48
Phyllotopsis nidulans, 164
Pisolithus tinctorius, *31*, 114
Polyozellus multiplex, 56, *134*
Polyporus
badius, 110, *148*
elegans, 110
brumalis, 164
melanopus, 111, *148*
picipes, 110
pubescens, 164
varius, 110
Psathyrella velutina, 93, *143*
Pulveroboletus ravenelii, 49
Pycnoporellus fulgens, 111, *148*
Pycnoporus
cinnabarinus, 112, *148*
sanguineus, 112, *149*
Ramaria
abietina, *29*, 59
fennica, 164
ochraceovirens, 59
sanguinea, 164
Russula ventricosipes, *27*, 94
Sarcodon
fuligineo-violaceus, 126, *152*
fuscoindicus, 126, *152*
imbricatus, 127, *152*
joeides, 127, *152*
scabrosus, 128, *152*
subincarnatus, 128, *152*
underwoodii, 129, *153*
Sarcodontia setosa, *31*, 60
Sarcoscypha austriaca, 164
Schizopora paradoxa, 98

Scleroderma
citrinum, 164
geaster, 115
macrorhizon, 114
meridionale, *31*, 114
polyrhizon, 115, *149*
Stereum
murraii, 60
tuberculosum, 60
Stropharia
ambigua, 94, *144*
rugosoannulata, 164
Suillus
americanus, 49
clintonianus, 52
cothurnatus, 50
granulatus, 51
grevillei, 51
grevillei var. *clintonianus*, 52
salmonicolor, 50, 164
Thelephora
anthocephala, 63
palmata, *29*, 63
terrestris, 63, *135*
terrestris f. *concrescens*, 64, *135*
vialis, *29*, 64
Trametes
cervina, 164
hirsuta, 113
pubescens, 113
versicolor, 113, *149*, *157*
Trichaptum biforme, 164
Tricholoma
aestuans, 164
vaccinum, 95, *144*
Tricholomopsis
decora, 164
rutilans, 95, *144*
sulfureoides, 164
Tubaria confragosa, 164
Tylopilus
alboater, 52
atronicotianus, 53
Tyromyces chioneus, 164
Xylaria polymorpha, 164

PHOTO CREDITS

Catherine Ardrey: *Cortinarius croceus, Cort. senguineus*
Dail Dunaway: *Inonotus hispidus*
Kenneth M. Evenson: *Hydnellum peckii*
Kenneth J. Harrison: *Hydnellum suaveolens, Phellodon alboniger, Phellodon tomentosus*
Emily Johnson: *Tricholomopsis rutilans*
Joe Liggio: *Phlebia incarnata*
Andrew Methven: *Clavariadelphus occidentalis*
Orson K. Miller, Jr.: *Phellodon atratus*
Sam Norris: Parts of the Mushroom drawing, p. 6
Bill Roody: *Clavariadelphus pistillaris, Tylopilus atronicotianus*
Walt Sundberg: *Polyozellus multiplex*
Steve Trudell: *Boletus aereus, Cortinarius phoeniceus* var. *occidentalis, Cortinarius sanguineus*

PHOTO PARTICIPANTS

Photographs of the following individuals are included in this book:

Mattias Andersson p. 20
Myra Beebee p. 14
Patricia Brannen p. 17 (L)
Jean Mounter p. 21
Samantha Noti p. 2
Patricia Olson p. 17 (R)
Trine Parmer p. 18
Margaret Trussell p. 12

ARLEEN RAINIS BESSETTE is a mycologist and botanical photographer, as well as a clinical psychologist, who has been collecting and studying wild mushrooms for several years. She has authored or coauthored five books including: *Taming the Wild Mushroom: A Culinary Guide to Market Foraging*, *Mushrooms of North America in Color*, *Mushrooms of Northeastern North America*, and *Wildflowers of New York in Color*. Arleen's most recent book is *North American Boletes—A Guide to the Fleshy Pored Mushrooms*. She has won several national awards for her photography, and teaches courses in mycology as well as mushroom dyeing workshops for the North American Mycological Association and other organizations.

ALAN BESSETTE is a mycologist and professor of biology at Utica College of Syracuse University. He has published numerous professional papers in the field of mycology and has authored or coauthored twelve books including: *Edible and Poisonous Mushrooms of New York*, *Mushrooms of the Adirondacks*, *Mushrooms: A Quick Reference Guide to Mushrooms of North America* and *Edible Wild Mushrooms of North America*. Alan has presented numerous mycological programs, is the scientific advisor to the Mid-York Mycological Society, and serves as a consultant for the New York State Poison Control Center. He has been the principal mycologist at national and regional forays and was the recipient of the 1987 Northeast Mycological Foray Service Award and the 1992 North American Mycological Association Award for Contributions to Amateur Mycology.